Revitalization Lexicography

Revitalization Lexicography

The Making of the New Tunica Dictionary

PATRICIA M. ANDERSON

THE UNIVERSITY OF
ARIZONA PRESS

TUCSON

The University of Arizona Press
www.uapress.arizona.edu

We respectfully acknowledge the University of Arizona is on the land and territories of Indigenous peoples. Today, Arizona is home to twenty-two federally recognized tribes, with Tucson being home to the O'odham and the Yaqui. The university strives to build sustainable relationships with sovereign Native Nations and Indigenous communities through education offerings, partnerships, and community service.

© 2020 by The Arizona Board of Regents
All rights reserved. Published 2020

ISBN-13: 978-0-8165-3959-8 (hardcover)
ISBN-13: 978-0-8165-5723-3 (paperback)
ISBN-13: 978-0-8165-4184-3 (ebook)

Cover design by Derek Thornton/Notch Design
Cover textures from Shutterstock
Interior design and typesetting by Sara Thaxton
Typeset in 10.25/15 Arno Pro (text) and Bulmer MT Std (display)

Publication of this book is made possible in part by the proceeds of a permanent endowment created with the assistance of a Challenge Grant from the National Endowment for the Humanities, a federal agency.

Library of Congress Cataloging-in-Publication Data
Names: Anderson, Patricia M., 1986– author.
Title: Revitalization lexicography : the making of the new Tunica dictionary / Patricia M. Anderson.
Description: Tucson : University of Arizona Press, 2020. | Includes bibliographical references and index.
Identifiers: LCCN 2020017605 | ISBN 9780816539598 (hardcover)
Subjects: LCSH: Tunica language—Lexicography. | Tunica language—Dictionaries—History.
Classification: LCC PM2498 .A53 2020 | DDC 497/.9—dc23
LC record available at https://lccn.loc.gov/2020017605

Printed in the United States of America
♾ This paper meets the requirements of ANSI/NISO Z39.48-1992 (Permanence of Paper).

For Speck and the next generation of Tunica speakers

Contents

Acknowledgments

This book has undergone many stages, and numerous people have supported my work through it in many ways. I want to first extend my deep appreciation to members of the Tunica-Biloxi Tribal Council and Language and Culture Revitalization Program: Brenda Lintinger, John Barbry, Donna Pierite, and Elisabeth Mora. You welcomed me into your classrooms, homes, and celebrations; and this work would not have been possible without your generosity and your tenacity in language revitalization. To Judith Maxwell, my graduate advisor and immersion camp companion, your pfannkuchen is nourishment for the soul, and your expertise continues to guide my scholarship in countless ways. My work and the New Tunica Dictionary were made richer by the wealth of knowledge and limitless dedication of Tunica teachers, Tunica learners, and Tulane students and faculty. Specifically, to the members of the Kuhpani Yoyani Luhchi Yoroni, thank you for your patience in tackling the fundamental questions of Tunica grammar and meaning as we wrestled with their representation in the dictionary. A special thanks to Dave Prine and Skye Anderson for undertaking the initial entry of Tunica legacy data. To my first summer camp students, whom I have watched grow in the language and their confidence these many years: each of you is a constant source of inspiration. The joy I have felt in pursuing the dictionary is compounded each time we greet each other in Tunica.

I spoke with several linguists, lexicographers, and community experts in pursuit of the New Tunica Dictionary, all of whom had valuable insight into our process:

Daryn McKenny, Nick Thieberger, Andrew Garret, Ann Bush, Jack Martin, Linda Langley, and Erin Debenport. Thank you for your time and words of advice. I want to thank the American Philosophical Society, which provided funding for my dissertation, on which this book is based. I am deeply grateful for the expertise of Brian Carpenter and Paul Sutherland at the Center for Native American and Indigenous Research, along with the enthusiastic interest of American Philosophical Society archivists Estelle Markel-Joyet and David Gary, all of whom were integral to exploring the depths of Mary R. Haas's uncatalogued collection.

Thank you to the readers of my earlier manuscript, who challenged me to frame technical linguistic concepts in nontechnical, accessible prose: Mark Zender and Olanikė Ola Orie. I would also like to thank those took time out of their busy schedules to review book chapters and manuscript drafts—Keren Rice and several anonymous reviewers—your detailed feedback enriched this book in many ways. To my amazing copyeditor, Jessica Hinds-Bond, you were able to draw concision from even my most meandering sentences, thank you. To my writing buddies, Joyce Bennet and Alli Carlisle, you both kept me sane and on track.

Finally, this work would not have been possible without my family: my parents, Catherine and David Anderson, thank you for supporting my endless curiosity in all things language and for instilling in me a lifelong love of learning; Speck, thank you for enforcing a fixed deadline; and Kirsten, thank you for your unwavering support.

Revitalization Lexicography

Chapter One

Revitalization Lexicography in Action

The conservation hall of the Tunica-Biloxi Cultural Education and Resources Center is abuzz with laughter and competition. One group of students is huddled over a fabric fishpond, goading their classmates to try and catch the *nini mili* instead of the *nini rɔwa* because red fish are much more desirable than the white ones. Another group is digging through a collection of old magazines, looking for the perfect bug picture to add to their *shila* collage. One of the students asks whether *shilakalu oni* is the right way to say Spider-Man. "Close," says the summer camp assistant. "It's switched. *Oni Shilakalu*." A third group, composed of more advanced speakers, is by far the most focused. Brows furrowed in concentration, they trade turns adding letters to a growing stack in the middle of the table. I head over to the third group and watch as they rearrange letters. The language learners are playing Rohina Luwa, a Tunica-language adaptation of Scrabble GO. "That's not a word!" asserts one of the players. The letters stacked in front of them spell out *naha*. The word's creator doesn't know what *naha* means, but he contends that it is real. With the word's validity challenged, another player produces a cell phone and navigates to the online Tunica dictionary. The debate is quickly settled. The word *is* in the dictionary: "to lean against something."

Many elements of the above scene have long been part of the morning precamp routine at the Tunica-Biloxi Language and Culture Summer Camp. However, the readily accessible online dictionary complete with Tunica words in contemporary orthography is a new addition and has measurably altered the ways in which Tunica learners interact with the language. Prior to 2017, lexical disagreements could only be settled by accessing a fragile, out-of-print copy of the *Tunica Dictionary* (Haas 1953), available for viewing at the Tunica library or through one of the Tunica language experts. Dictionary in hand, the inquirer could then look up the English word in the perfunctory English–Tunica index, before flipping to the Tunica–English portion of the dictionary to get any sort of context clues or disambiguation of the term. This clunky and inexact method meant that Tunica learners would instead shy away from using new or unfamiliar language for fear they were using it "wrong" and express the feeling that Tunica was too hard to learn because they couldn't figure out what words meant.

Tunica, one of the heritage languages of the Tunica-Biloxi Tribe of Marksville, Louisiana, has been undergoing active revitalization since 2010. The current generation of speakers began learning Tunica, a once-sleeping language, through written documentation. Almost ten years later, there are now enough Tunica speakers to confer among themselves when questionable language use arises; however, a strong penchant remains for verifying most language use by consulting written texts. This predisposition has driven community interest in the app and online forms of the New Tunica Dictionary, the advent of which has resulted in Tunica speakers much more willing to produce the language.

The New Tunica Dictionary, an ongoing project as of 2020, was and continues to be an incredible investment of time and resources on the part of the Tunica Language Project (TLP). The TLP is a community-driven language revitalization effort owned and directed by the Tunica-Biloxi Tribe; which is to say that while anyone associated with the TLP can propose revitalization ideas and projects they'd like to work on, community-proposed initiatives are given priority and Tunica-Biloxi leadership ultimately determines which proposals are pursued. In its early stages, the TLP worked to revitalize the language as recorded in three published works by Mary R. Haas, a meticulous scholar who documented the language of the last known native Tunica speaker,[1] Sesostrie Youchigant. These works

---

1. The author is fully aware that the concept of "last native speaker" is a both arbitrary and problematic in the revitalization arena. Nicholas Evans (2001) demonstrates how definitions of speakerhood shift as the language situation shifts, and nonlinguistic determinations, such as intragroup politics or social affiliations, can influence who is bestowed the title of speaker. What's more, external researchers can fail to acknowledge speakers who do not fit a Western

were difficult for nonlinguists to understand: the orthography, or writing system, was APA;[2] sentences were recorded with phrase breaks in lieu of word breaks; concepts such as durativity and transimpersonal verbs were strewn throughout the texts with little explanation as to their meaning. The TLP prioritized updating these older Tunica materials and making them available for community consumption. Children's stories were adapted from *Tunica Texts* (Haas 1950), converted into the contemporary orthography, and distributed by the Tribe to Tunica-Biloxi households (KYLY 2011, KYLY forthcoming). The Tunica grammar (Haas 1940) was contemporized and disseminated through a variety of media. From new pedagogical materials to online games teaching Tunica phonology to an introductory Tunica textbook (KYLY forthcoming), Tunica grammar in abridged and unabridged formats is available to teachers, linguists, and learners. I worked on many of these projects as a graduate student affiliated with Tulane University, a collaborative partner with the TLP since its inception. As the project continued to unfold, the desire for an updated dictionary was regularly remarked, but resources, both financial and personnel, were initially too limited for such an undertaking. When the time came to declare my dissertation topic in 2013, I asked members of the TLP and Tunica-Biloxi leadership in what way my dissertation could be most useful to the community. The answer was unanimous; it was time for an updated Tunica dictionary.

I worked on the New Tunica Dictionary full time from 2013 to 2017 and continue to work with the TLP in efforts to finalize the dictionary for print and digital publication; I was not the sole contributor to the dictionary, but as head lexicographer I drafted proposals for dictionary structure, format, and content; and I organized community and noncommunity member tasks from data entry to example sentence construction. I selected dictionary software, ran trainings and workshops

---

cultural definition of speakerhood (Leonard and Haynes 2010), and declarations of a "last speaker" may evoke a finality akin to language death, barring the possibility of any future native speakers (Davis 2017). That said, Tunica speakers often use the phrase "last native speaker" to describe Youchigant because of his unique contribution to the Tunica revitalization process. This designation does not, in the eyes of the community, bar future native speakers; and when talking about Youchigant, speakers often say that he was the last native speaker but that "we are getting closer every day."

2. APA stands for (North) American Phonetic Alphabet, also known as Americanist Phonetic Notation. This phonetic alphabet was particularly popular among American linguists at the turn of the twentieth century.

on how to work with various lexicographic tools, and conducted pilot tests of dictionary apps. I started this project thinking dictionary construction would be largely mechanical, entering headwords into digital software and all the while eliciting consensus from the group on the final content and dictionary format. Yet, as I worked on the New Tunica Dictionary, I quickly realized that a dictionary is more than just a collection of words. Dictionaries are bestowed a sense of authority over the languages they encode. Consequently, decisions made to include or exclude certain language and language representation have reverberating consequences in the eyes of the larger community. My job as head lexicographer evolved far beyond the responsibility of inputting words and selecting fonts. Rather, I guided members of the TLP in explicitly outlining how the language ideology of the group would be represented to the larger community through the dictionary. Ideologies, or "beliefs and feelings about language" (Kroskrity and Field 2009, 4), were highlighted with questions: What constitutes "authentic" Tunica, and how are forms deemed less authentic represented in the dictionary, if at all? Do expressed learner needs such as morphologically transparent forms take precedent over attested forms in historical contexts? If yes, how are these new and old forms represented in the dictionary? What kinds of example sentences are appropriate for dictionary entries? As speakers learn more Tunica and consequently change certain phonological structures, should the dictionary hold firm in emphasizing the previous, more complex structures, or should it document and describe the changes speakers are making to the language today? In what ways should the dictionary standardize the language, and where should it celebrate diverse language representation? Much time was spent negotiating intragroup differences in language ideologies and building consensus about how the differences would be represented in a reference work. Ultimately, my job as head lexicographer hinged on guiding the TLP in clarifying its overall revitalization goals and suggesting avenues through which the dictionary could support these goals.

This book details the creation of the New Tunica Dictionary: the challenges we faced, the decisions we made, and the ultimate outcome. It covers topics both practical and theoretical in the creation of dictionaries. Universally applicable lexicographic topics related to dictionary planning and compilation are explained throughout. However, I spend extra time and attention discussing how the creation of the New Tunica Dictionary was leveraged to advance the larger revitalization project. While many dictionary-building considerations hold true for lexicography in all language contexts, others do not; "traditional" lexicographic quandaries such as how to handle new words or the extent to which grammatical information should be included in a dictionary are considered differently in the context of an active language revitalization movement. Throughout the book, I will home in on activities that facilitated both the completion of the New Tunica Dictionary and the advancement of Tunica language revitalization, a hybrid venture I call revitalization lexicography.

Revitalization lexicography seeks to use dictionaries and dictionary-making processes to reverse language shift. Revitalization lexicography includes the explicit acknowledgment that collecting, cataloging, and organizing language is not a neutral act, and that the way in which said lexicography is conducted has material impact on language use, perceptions, and attitudes. Contemporary Western lexicographers generally eschew influencing language through the dictionaries they produce, even though, as we shall see in chapter 2, this attitude has not been consistent through history nor fully achieved by modern dictionaries. Revitalization lexicographers, in contrast, recognize that their work can and should affect language use, and they openly solicit community-based language activists' input on how a dictionary should wield its influence. Implicit in revitalization lexicography is the recognition that creating or possessing a dictionary is doubtless insufficient to revitalize a language on its own. I believe that revitalization lexicography is only ethical and effective if it is undertaken as part of a larger community-driven revitalization movement. It is one tool of many that can move the needle forward on revitalization. Throughout this book, I interweave discussion on the ways in which lexicographic activities can be aligned with speaker and community needs for a cohesive revitalization effort.

I have designed this book to be the resource I wish I'd had when creating the New Tunica Dictionary. While existing guides to lexicography helped me consider topics such as how the competing halves of a bilingual dictionary interact with each other—or what the broader consequences might be of labeling a word "obsolete" versus "archaic" (versus using no label whatsoever)—I regularly faced lexicographic questions specific to our community and for which I could not find easy answers. For instance, I work with a geographically diffuse team with various levels of technological know-how; what software is best for our task? Less concrete queries also arose. The New Tunica Dictionary is designed to standardize not just orthographies, but entire grammatical features heretofore unpublished and unattested; what are best lexicographic practices in this situation? I could find no comprehensive resource that encompassed both practical and theoretical aspects of Indigenous-language lexicography in a revitalization context. I was ultimately able to answer these questions by leveraging personal and institutional privilege, accessing scientific journals and travel funding afforded me by my graduate program, which offset the cost of visits to archives, conferences, and professional meetings for face-to-face discussions with experienced lexicographers. The Tunica-Biloxi Tribe also expended resources on my behalf, sponsoring attendance to regional revitalization workshops and making introductions to experts in area communities. All this is to say that, in the end, I was able to find answers, but that a significant investment of time, money, and trial and error was needed to arrive at our final dictionary product. I know from my history with the TLP that resources are precious, and that time and manpower are valuable.

My goal is to share with the reader how we at the TLP tackled lexicographic issues at linguistic and community levels, to share which issues snuck up on us unexpectedly, and which we got unnecessarily worked up about, wasting resources of time and energy combating anticipated issues that never reared their heads. I would like the immense capital invested in pursuing the New Tunica Dictionary to benefit revitalization dictionaries beyond our own, to contribute to *inksehiti mashuwan* 'building our future' beyond the work of one language revitalization project.

I deeply understand that what worked for us and our language context is not a one-size-fits-all solution for anyone undertaking a dictionary for language revitalization. My work is by no means a sole replacement for all the work that has come before me and all that will come after. Language revitalization is a powerful undertaking, one that should be firmly under the control of the people whose language is being revitalized. I invite the reader to pass over any aspects of this book that are not relevant to their project or community. The context in which the Tunica language is being revitalized is specific to the Tunica-Biloxi Tribe and the state of the Tunica language. However, I hope that our journey is useful in your own understanding of the larger context of lexicography, the influential role that dictionaries play in our perceptions of language, the social connections that dictionaries can facilitate, and some of the nitty-gritty practicalities of Indigenous-language lexicography. All information divulged in this book is done with the full knowledge and approval of the Tunica-Biloxi Tribe. The Tunica people are proud of their language and of the strides they have made in relearning it. One way they wish to express their pride is by sharing their experience and their language with others. It is my privilege to document the lexicographic part of their journey here.

Learning from Existing Lexicographic Resources

The New Tunica Dictionary is not the first dictionary created by and for a community undertaking language revitalization, and it will not be the last. In seeking guidance on how to create an Indigenous-language dictionary, I drew on the widespread expertise of existing dictionaries, communities, linguistics, and lexicographers. I found that existing Indigenous-language dictionaries sometimes include treasure troves of information about their process in the front matter (e.g., Chinuk Wawa Dictionary Project 2012; Montler 2012; Quintero 2014). However, the inclusion of explicit information about the dictionary compilation process does not appear to be the norm, and the linguistics-based tradition of confining the front matter of a dictionary to a sketch grammar prevails in most cases.

Publications provided another avenue of learning about Indigenous-language dictionary creation. The available body of work largely consists of academic articles that, per their genre, are generally narrow in scope. Examples include articles by Ivy Doak and Timothy Montler (2000), who describe the Coeur d'Alene Dictionaries Project's approach to orthography, and Margaret C. Field (2009), who discusses polysemy and the structure of entries and subentries in Navajo dictionaries. These articles contributed to TLP discussions of formatting and headword representation in the New Tunica Dictionary. Articles describing digital lexicography of Indigenous languages have been published, such as Aidan Wilson's (2010) description of Kaurna and Wagiman digital dictionaries and Inge Genee and Marie-Odile Junker's (2018) account of the Blackfoot Language Resources and Digital Dictionary project; these accounts document the work that has long been ongoing in language communities and were helpful in imagining how we would shape our digital Tunica dictionary. While several formerly sleeping languages—Wampanoag, Mutsun, and Myaamia, among others—have produced dictionaries, Mutsun was the only one on which I could find published insight into its lexicographic processes. Natasha Warner, Lynnika Butler, and Quirina Luna-Costillas (2006), Warner, Luna, and Butler (2007), and Warner et al. (2009) outline several tactics in their approach to revitalizing Mutsun from archival materials and discuss concrete decisions of orthography, morphology, and grammatical information included in the new Mutsun dictionary.

A highly nuanced account of making a dictionary with an Indigenous community is found in the work of Erin Debenport (2015). Her chapter on Keiwa example sentence creation as the embodiment of language ideology directly influenced conversations about Tunica example sentence creation. Other works that shed light on aspects of Indigenous-language lexicography are those by William J. Frawley, Kenneth C. Hill, and Pamela Munro (2002) and Sarah Ogilvie (2011a); these resources devote themselves entirely to Indigenous-language lexicography and are helpful in identifying how Indigenous-language lexicography deviates from Western lexicography. In addition to Indigenous lexicography resources, I consulted several "standard" lexicography manuals to guide my work, including texts from Ladislav Zgusta (1971), Bo Svensén (1993), and Piet van Sterkenburg (2003).

Why Make a Dictionary?

The question "why make a dictionary?" may seem banal but spending time with this typically unexamined inquiry grants insight into the unique space that dictionaries occupy in the larger social imaginary. I have yet to meet a revitalization community that does not have its eyes on a dictionary: either it already has a dictionary, it is actively undertaking a dictionary, or it desperately wants a dictionary. Dictionary creation is a time-consuming, resource-intensive process, yet broad groups such as language communities, academics, and funding organizations all agree that dictionaries are worthwhile investments. What elements of dictionaries make them so universally appealing?

The history of using dictionaries to preserve and promote language dates to the early twentieth century, when dictionaries accounted for one-third of the Boasian trinity of language documentation, accompanying a grammar and a compilation of language texts. In a linguistic climate that is hyperaware of the perils of so-called language death (Crystal 2000; Nettle and Romaine 2002; UNESCO 2003), dictionaries are touted as stalwarts in preventing a language from vanishing from human history. Online dictionaries, talking dictionaries, print dictionaries, dictionary apps for phones, and dictionary games have all been funded by organizations such as the Living Tongues Institute, the Endangered Language Fund, the Summer Institute of Linguistics (now SIL International), the National Science Foundation, National Geographic Society, and countless universities. These dictionaries not only preserve language, they also document cultural and social practices that are falling out of use (Cablitz 2011). While dictionaries on their own do not contain enough information to drive language revitalization, their reputation as multifunctional reference material makes them adaptable to a variety of language community needs. The centrality of a dictionary to language revitalization is especially apparent when revitalizing a language that has no native speakers; in this context, a language learner does not have the luxury of asking her elders "how do you say _____?" Instead, learners turn to a dictionary to build their vocabulary and facilitate language production.

Dictionaries are often viewed as unquestioned wellsprings of legitimate language use or unbiased arbiters of good and bad speech. Dictionaries have been granted final say on "proper" language. If a speaker, even a native speaker, uses a word that is not found in the dictionary, people are more likely to question the legitimacy of the speaker than the legitimacy of the dictionary. The authority associated with dictionaries imparts prestige to any language that has one; and a language with a dictionary is deemed more "legitimate" by both speakers and nonspeakers alike. One concrete example of this legitimacy is the manner in which Native American dictionaries are cited in appeals for federal recognition in the United States, as was seen in the Tunica-Biloxi petition; a dictionary qualifies as evidence to an outside government that the group has long been a sovereign nation.

This very curious phenomenon of lexicographic authority, one that did not happen by accident, will be explored in chapter 2. As we shall see, the history and practice of practical lexicography render it impossible for dictionaries to be impartial texts. Yet, the truth that dictionaries are narrative works is obfuscated by the societal pedestal on which we place the dictionary. So ubiquitous is the dictionary that we overlook the reality that it is a series of decisions made by people at a specific point in history with identifiable goals and desired outcomes. Rather than being objective, all dictionaries of all languages are embodiments of the creators' language ideology. In chapters 3 and 4, I outline the ways in which the Tunica dictionary embodies ideologies espoused by the TLP. Chapter 3 specifically highlights precompilation planning decisions made for the New Tunica Dictionary and their long-term implications, while chapter 4 focuses on decisions affected by dictionary structure. Wielding its power for encoding language ideology, a dictionary can be designed to encourage one kind of language use over another. The treatment of neologisms in a dictionary provides concrete insight into this objective; headword choice can legitimize neologisms in expanded domains or encourage speakers to honor traditional language use. Chapter 5 discusses neologisms in the New Tunica Dictionary and the ways in which the dictionary-building process was leveraged to expand Tunica into new domains.

Dictionaries have many uses and roles in a language community; their incredible social versatility is part of their widespread appeal. Dictionaries are authoritative resources on a language to tell a speaker how a language is or is not used; dictionaries are markers of legitimacy, demonstrating to outsiders and speakers alike that the language is sophisticated enough to deserve a dictionary; dictionaries preserve and document culture tied to vocabulary no longer used by speakers; dictionaries are used to teach, demonstrating that the language is approachable and learnable; dictionaries, especially technical dictionaries, are used to show the modernity of a language. All other uses of dictionaries notwithstanding, my favorite description of dictionaries' role comes from Lynda Mugglestone (2011), who acknowledges that dictionaries are social and cultural products of the people who made them and the time they were made in; as such, dictionaries narrate a story of how the lexicographer wants others to see the language. The Tunica people wanted a dictionary that told the story "Our language was not spoken thirty years ago. But it is spoken now. And we will not be ignored." The desire to tell this story is implicit throughout the New Tunica Dictionary, and the experience of the community telling this story incontrovertibly influenced the final output of the Tunica dictionary process.

The Tunica People and Their Language

The Tunica-Biloxi have a long history of asserting their identities as autonomous peoples. They have been federally recognized since 1981, and they are some of the earliest inland Native peoples documented on the European record. The Tunica were initially encountered by Hernando de Soto in 1541 and dealt the Spanish their first recorded defeat at Quizquiz, a community unearthed in present-day Tennessee (Brain 1988). De Soto later met the "Tanico" near what is now Arkansas/

northern Louisiana. Scholars do not agree on whether the Tanico and the Tunica are one and the same (Brain 1988; Kniffen, Gregory, and Stokes 1994; Jeter 2002); regardless, in neither encounter was any language recorded.

The earliest archaeological records pertaining to the Tunica people indicate that the Tunica were extremely influential in the southeastern United States. Their prominence was largely attributed to their position as salt traders, acting as the primary middlemen between Caddoan salt producers and peoples farther inland (Brain 1977; Brown 1981). After European contact, the Tunica transitioned their prowess as salt traders to the trade of European valuables, leveraging their widespread trade networks to capitalize on Native American demand for horses (Brain 1990). Their dominance in the region positioned the Tunica to be strong allies of the French; indeed, one observer of the nineteenth-century French and Tunica interactions stated that it was difficult to assess who influenced the other more (Kniffen, Gregory, and Stokes 1994, 211). During this time, Jesuit missionaries settled among the Tunica people, who had moved south to the Yazoo River along the modern Louisiana-Mississippi border. Letters that date as early as 1700 outlining missionary work and ethnographic information were sent by Father Antoine Davion[3] to the seminary in Quebec, where they reside today. The TLP has acquired much of Father Davion's correspondence but unfortunately has yet to find any Tunica language in the documents. Father Davion lived among the Tunica and Yazoo peoples for more than twenty years, until he was recalled to France in 1725 (Thwaites 1896).

The Tunica alliance with the French led to recognition by the French government, and later the Spanish government, of the Tunica as a sovereign people. The Spanish officially recognized the Tunica's homeland with a large land grant in 1779 (Downs 1979). The original land grant, in present-day central Louisiana, far exceeded the bounds of the contemporary reservation. Immediately following the Louisiana Purchase, the Tunica people attempted to garner the same recognition from the United States government; their first petition was filed in 1826 (Klopotek 2011). However, the Tunica peoples were written off by Dr. John Sibley, who was appointed by President Thomas Jefferson to determine the state of affairs with southeastern Indian tribes. Sibley (1832, 725) wrote: "These people formerly lived

---

3. While history books record him as Antoine Davion, the Séminaire de Québec Archives have his records filed under the name David Davion.

on the Bayou Tunica, above Point Coupeé, on the Mississippi, Eastside; live now at Avoyelles; do not, at present, exceed twenty-five men. Their native language is peculiar to themselves, but speak Mobilian; are employed occasionally by the inhabitants as boatmen, etc., in amity with all other people, and gradually diminishing in numbers." The U.S. government denied their petition for recognition and hoped that the Tunica would soon vanish. However, the Tunica did quite the opposite, as evidenced by their tireless lawsuits, petitions, and appeals throughout the nineteenth and twentieth centuries to fight the encroachment of white settlers and townspeople. The Tunica-Biloxi Tribe won state recognition in 1975 and federal recognition in 1981.[4]

Today, the Tunica-Biloxi Tribe has approximately 1,300 enrolled members. Half of the enrolled members live within forty miles of the reservation, located in north central Louisiana. However, stark economic isolation present before federal recognition drove many families to look for work away from their established homeland. As a result, roughly one-half of enrolled members reside farther off-rez, in Houston and Chicago. Enrolled members are active within the Tribe regardless of geographic location. Many members return to the reservation on a regular basis for larger tribal events, such as the annual pow-wow, all-community political gatherings, or language summer camps.

Tunica Language Record

Despite the substantial recorded history of the Tunica people dating from the infancy of inland European military expeditions, no Tunica language was recorded outright. Toponyms of known Tunica settlements, such as Quizquiz, are not likely of Tunica origin.[5] While interactions with Tunica chiefs are mentioned in historical texts, few are named. The first undoubtedly Tunica chiefs to enter the European historical record are Cahura Joligo and his successor, Bride les Boeuf (Batz 1732). Again, the origin of these names is unclear; both are clearly influenced by French, as the /g/ of "Joligo" is not a phoneme native to Tunica, and "les Boeuf" is

---

4. A detailed account of the entire Tunica-Biloxi recognition process can be found in Klopotek (2011).

5. Scholars agree that "Quizquiz" does not sound like a Tunica name (Jeter 2002), though they do not agree on the toponym's language of origin. Swanton (1911) hypothesized that Quizquiz was a Natchez word.

clearly of French origin. Whether these words were Frenchified versions of Tunica names or taken directly from the French, we cannot know. To this day, most names seen on the Tunica-Biloxi tribal rolls are of English, French, or Spanish origin. Several centuries of Tunica-European interaction passed before the first known Tunica-language documents appeared in 1886.

Three scholars documented Tunica before the language fell temporarily dormant. Traveling scholar Albert S. Gatschet (1886b) announced his "discovery" of the language in 1886. Gatschet's original "discovery" letter sits in the National Anthropological Archives today, alongside a 256-page handwritten grammar of Tunica, and stories that William Ely Johnson recounted to him in Tunica. John R. Swanton was head of the Bureau of American Ethnology in the early twentieth century and, as such, had access to Gatschet's original materials. Swanton was interested in collecting more Tunica and made several trips to Louisiana between 1907 and 1910. Swanton worked primarily with then chief Volsin Chiki and the chief's nephew Sesostrie Youchigant, also known as Sam Young. Johnson also worked with Swanton during this time. Swanton gathered more stories, but the bulk of his work was typing and organizing Gatschet's materials. One such project was the creation of more than three thousand vocabulary cards in preparation for a Tunica dictionary that was never published.

In the 1930s, Mary R. Haas arrived in Marksville as a young graduate student studying linguistics under Edward Sapir. She was tasked with creating a complete description of the Tunica language, working with Youchigant, by that time the only remaining speaker and a former Tunica chief. Youchigant and Haas worked together for just two summers, but they recorded incredible amounts of the language. They also made recordings of the language, which can be heard online via the California Language Archive.[6] Haas published a Tunica grammar in 1940, the book *Tunica Texts* in 1950, and the *Tunica Dictionary* in 1953.

Various secondary sources containing Tunica language have cropped up over the years, including texts by Kunihiko Ogawa (1971), Marianne Mithun (1999), Wendy J. Wiswall (1991), and Hua Lin (2003). Tunica's unique linguistic features coupled with Haas's extremely detailed grammar have inspired authors to

---

6. The California Language Archive is an online tool of the Survey of California and Other Indian Languages, at the University of California, Berkeley. The website address is http://cla .berkeley.edu/.

include the language as a data set in their publications. Tunica has several interesting phonological features, such as translaryngeal vowel harmony. The Tunica language shares areal features—such as subject-object-verb word order, the use of positional verbs as existentials, and active-stative alignment—with other languages of the southeastern United States (Heaton 2016; Anderson 2017). Tunica also encodes several unique elements, such as a robust grammatical gender in second and third person, a feature that is highly unusual among North American languages (Mithun 1999). Grammatical gender is encoded on nouns and through verb agreement. The gender-number suffixes found in Tunica mark grammatical gender and distinguish between single, dual, and, plural; gender-number suffixes also cross the boundary into animacy class, distinguishing inanimate objects and animals from humans. All these Tunica feature sets have been explored in the aforementioned papers, but these publications rely solely on Haas's texts as a source of information. While the papers bring important analysis to the field of academic linguistics, they do not evidence any previously undocumented Tunica language. For all intents and purposes, Tunica was a sleeping language from the middle of the twentieth century until the contemporary revitalization project began in 2010.

Tunica Language Revitalization

The death of Sesostrie Youchigant in 1948 (Pierite 1964) ushered in a period of Tunica language dormancy. During this time, Tunica heritage speakers retained some emblematic phrases, such as *lapuhch,* "it would be a good thing." In the 1990s, Donna Pierite and her family were designated Tunica storytellers and legend keepers and, as such, began performing Tunica stories as dictated to Haas and recorded in *Tunica Texts* (Anderson and Maxwell 2019). However, spontaneous Tunica language production did not begin anew until the establishment of the TLP.

The TLP began in 2010, when Tunica-Biloxi councilwoman Brenda Lintinger reached out to Dr. Judith Maxwell of the Tulane University linguistics program. Lintinger had access to the Haas materials and had attempted to construct new Tunica phrases by referencing Haas; but Haas had written her books with a technical audience in mind, and Lintinger ultimately felt she needed reinforcements with a technical linguistics background to aid in deciphering and interpreting the older materials. Maxwell immediately affirmed this as a community-driven process and worked with the Tunica-Biloxi to identify community language goals and needs. With an expressed desire to elevate an Indigenous sense of self by making the Tunica language visible to tribal and nontribal community members alike, Tunica leadership identified several concrete objectives for the infant language revitalization project: reinstitute ritualized Tunica for opening ceremonies and important gatherings, display the Tunica language more prominently in public spaces on the reservation, and contemporize existing Tunica-language documents for consumption by the Tunica community (Maxwell, Anderson, and Heaton 2017). In its first year, the TLP wrote a Tunica prayer, published a children's book from previously recorded Tunica stories, and created a number of pedagogical materials for Tunica teachers. All projects drew from the set of Tunica-language materials produced by Gatschet, Swanton, and Haas. As the TLP continued its revitalization project, it acquired access to more legacy materials penned by these authors, including wax cylinder recordings of the language, handwritten field notes, and unpublished grammars buried deep within uncatalogued archives. As the project grew, the TLP established a working group, the Kuhpani Yoyani Luhchi Yoroni (KYLY), to meet regularly via online video chat and in-person meetings to advance the projects of the TLP.

The Tribe officially established a language revitalization program in 2012. The Language and Culture Revitalization Program (LCRP) is funded by the Tribe with the explicit mission to revitalize language and cultural practices. In addition to language, the LCRP advances the revitalization of cultural activities such as basket weaving and stickball. Tunica is currently the only heritage language undergoing active revitalization, even though Biloxi, Ofo, and Avoylle are also heritage languages of the Tunica-Biloxi Tribe.[7] The Tunica-Biloxi language immersion camp for young Tunica learners has been held annually since 2012. The number of participants grows each year, with more than sixty students registered in 2018; several students travel from Houston and Chicago to participate. A separate annual immersion workshop for Tunica teachers, advanced teenage speakers, and

---

7. Some tribal members also consider Louisiana French to be a heritage language. French education is promoted in Louisiana public and private schools, supported through the Council for the Development of French in Louisiana (CODOFIL 2017). School-aged Tunica-Biloxi members have exposure to French through these programs, though CODOFIL consistently comes under fire for hiring European French speakers rather than educators of Louisiana French (Ross et al. 2018).

tribal staff garners strong participation. The Tribe won a multi-year grant from the Administration for Native Americans in 2018; the grant funds the training of five full-time language apprentices, whom the Tribe expects to become the next generation of Tunica language teachers. All told, approximately ten speakers can speak Tunica with advanced proficiency, more than twenty-five speakers are conversational, and more than fifty speakers are familiar with greetings and basic vocabulary.

The Tunica Working Group and Self-Location of the Author

The Tunica working group, referred to throughout this book as KYLY, consists of nearly two dozen Tunica-Biloxi and non-Tunica-Biloxi participants. Tribe-affiliated Tunica-Biloxi membership has consistently grown from year to year since Tunica revitalization began. Tunica-Biloxi members include teachers, staff members, and language apprentices. In contrast, Tulane membership has remained numerically consistent; a handful of Tulane students rotate on or off the project as they move through their studies, excepting approximately six Tulane-affiliated KYLY members who have remained consistent over the years.

The physical distance between the Tribe's reservation in Marksville, Louisiana, and Tulane's campus in New Orleans (a one-way trip takes approximately three hours by car) necessitates that most collaboration take place via online meeting spaces, such as Google Hangouts. KYLY has grown large enough that subgroups have been formed to tackle individual projects, with a biweekly "all-hands" meeting to present progress and discuss questions or challenges. Larger projects are chosen on a yearly basis, often coinciding with the start of a new academic year; these might include preparing a new grammar textbook or heightening the language program's social media presence. When smaller, finite projects pop up throughout the year, interested subgroups will generally take charge of them. For example, one year, the neologisms subgroup translated a number of Christmas carols into the Tunica; the larger all-hands group reviewed the translations and discussed the proposed neologisms. Tulane members of KYLY travel to Marksville two to four times per year for immersion workshops, language camps, and special events hosted by the Tribe such as basket-weaving seminars or the annual pow-wow.

I, the author, am a non-Indigenous academic who started my graduate studies at Tulane University in 2011, just one year after the TLP began. I had not intended to join the revitalization effort when I enrolled at Tulane. Instead, I was volun-told for the joint collaboration when I made the mistake of telling my advisor, Dr. Maxwell, that I was enjoying having "more free time than I expected" my first semester in graduate school. She promptly assigned me to the TLP. It was the best and most rewarding slip of the tongue I have ever made in my academic career. I worked with the TLP through the completion of my PhD in 2017; I have remained active in the group, participating in weekly online meetings and contributing to the ongoing production of lexicographic and pedagogical materials.

In addition to pursuing a graduate degree in linguistic anthropology, I have long had a penchant for dissecting technology. I see the two interests as related; language and technology are both tools that humans use to interact with their environments, to extract meaning about and value from the world around them. I enjoy finding avenues in which technology enhances or eases people's day-to-day tasks. My proclivity for useful technology started early; in middle school, I would reset blinking clocks on VCRs whenever I walked into a room, and as personal computers became a household commodity in my high school years, I was always happy to help folks install, troubleshoot, or improve their interactions with their software. I became interested enough in technology that I taught myself to code in graduate school, and I worked part time at a technology company as a software engineer.

I mention this background because my technical bend undoubtably influenced the path the Tunica dictionary project took. In the twenty-first century, all dictionary creation is facilitated by software. I recognize that technology can be a daunting hurdle for many language activists. For me, technology was not a barrier in deciding the tools used by the Tunica dictionary project. I felt confident in my ability to evaluate technological tools, and my technical expertise granted me insight into which technologies' limitations I could compensate for with scripts or developer collaboration. Despite my confidence in interacting with dictionary software, my close ties with KYLY prior to becoming a lexicographer informed my technology decisions; a community-driven approach dictated that any work on the New Tunica Dictionary could be picked up by another collaborator as needed, and that technology should not be a barrier to that transfer. I was not the sole or even primary contributor to the dictionary. More importantly, I would not own the final product, and I would not be the one to maintain it long term. Before a single lexical item was inputted, the tenets of community-driven research heavily informed all aspects of Tunica language revitalization. My lexicographic decisions were shaped by the methodological context in which the New Tunica Dictionary was born.

Methodological Approach to the New Tunica Dictionary

The TLP has been firmly rooted in community-driven research (CDR) since its inception. Community-driven research is defined by Bertney Langley et al. (2018, 145) as "research which is driven entirely by the language community . . . the community decides what research is needed and seeks out specific researchers to provide expertise." CDR falls under the umbrella of the robust community-*based* research methodology, and as such CDR and community-based research share many features.[8] I will delve into the differences between these two approaches later in this section, but let's start with the similarities.

The Centre for Community-Based Research Canada describes the core principles of community-based research as (1) community relevance of research projects, (2) collaboration, and (3) action orientation (as cited in Rice 2018, 14). Defining features of the methodology include the following:

- the community identifies or verifies the value of research topics
- the research is accessible to the community as it is undertaken and when it is completed
- community expertise is both acknowledged and utilized throughout the research
- empowerment, social change, and respect for diversity drive the research process (Rice 2018, 15)

Community-based research departs from historical research methodologies in substantial ways, not least of which is the centrality of the community collaboration. Ewa Czaykowska-Higgins (2009, 17) defines community-based research

---

8. For an in-depth treatment of community-based research from a range of authors, see Bischoff and Jany (2018).

as being "for, with, and by community members" and states that researchers "are partners working in a collaborative relationship with members of the language-using community." Community involvement in projects that the community identifies as relevant leads to better research and ensures long-term project sustainability.[9] Researcher-driven projects are kept in motion only as long as the researcher remains involved. Once the researcher departs, for whatever reason, the project can easily wane. Researcher ownership of a project ties its fate to the tenure of the scholar. And all outside researchers eventually leave; funding dries up, new academic positions shift research priorities, or a researcher may simply burn out. Even in the rare case that a single researcher can devote a lifetime to working on a community-research project, occasionally feasible when the researcher is from the community, successful language revitalization spans generations.

This shift to a collaborative methodological approach is significant, as the scientific community has a sordid past in regard to research on Indigenous and Native American peoples. Many early imperial encounters with Indigenous peoples in the United States occurred under the guise of research. President Thomas Jefferson sent out expeditions to gather information about geography, flora and fauna, and Indigenous peoples and languages, the most famous of these being the Lewis and Clark Corps of Discovery expedition (1804–6). However, the rhetoric of discovery could not conceal the fact that the primary aim of these expeditions was to gather military intelligence on Native American peoples (Medlicott 2003). Scientific research was also used to establish non-Native land ownership claims in the early United States. For example, Albert Gallatin was interested in uncovering the affinities between different Native American languages, which led to the publication of *A Synopsis of the Indian Tribes of North America* (Gallatin 1836). However, his drive to categorize Native languages was not innocuous, as Kelly Wisecup (2016, 2) notes: "Linguistic collection was, for Gallatin and other U.S. men, not simply an activity that would provide insight into North America's past; it formed the foundation for theories about the relations between language and land, assumptions that supported efforts to remove Native people from their ancestral homelands." Given the track record of outsider-driven research, Māori scholar Linda Tuhiwai Smith (2012, 1) aptly states that "the word 'research' itself

---

9. For examples of the ways in which community-based research leads to better science, see Rice (2011).

is probably one of the dirtiest words in the indigenous world's vocabulary . . . inextricably linked to European imperialism and colonialism."

While more recent academic endeavors have not been as explicitly steeped in an imperial agenda, I agree with Wesley Y. Leonard (2018, 61) that "colonialism is so engrained in the academy that abolishing it is difficult, even when doing so arguably leads to better science." Indeed, Western academic institutions continue to reward extractive practices, particularly in regard to publication requirements for tenure and promotion.[10] In extractive methodologies, communities are treated as resource wells of data; the raw Indigenous knowledge is processed into westernized frameworks and synthesized for noncommunity audiences, and it is then published and archived in ways that make it inaccessible to the community. The work may be inaccessible for several reasons: it could be published in a language that the community does not speak; the work may be filled with terminology that is overly technical and without context for nonacademic community members; or the work may be archived in a physical location that is impractical to travel to in order to retrieve it. The rapid decline in the number of Indigenous-language speakers (Crystal 2000; Nettle and Romaine 2002) has further complicated the community-researcher dynamic, as it has motivated a set of outside researchers to rush around "salvaging" languages before they are lost forever. This patronizing approach assumes that the communities have neither agency nor ownership over the fate of their language.[11]

Community-based research has many methodological peers outside the academic fields of anthropology and linguistics: participatory action research (Benedicto 2018), public scholarship (Krabill 2012), collaborative community scholarship, and community-based participatory research (Postma 2008, Shore et al. 2008), to name but a few. Community-engaged scholarship also falls within this realm and encompasses a direct call to academic institutions to formally recognize work done in partnership with communities (Saltmarsh et al. 2009). Many of these methodologies, including community-based research, have a distinct aspect in common: they call on academics—framed as noncommunity researchers—to ensure that collaboration and respect are at the forefront of their work.

---

10. For an excellent analysis of how Western academic institutions maintain researcher-community power imbalances by means of controlling publications standards, see Benedicto (2018).

11. For more on language ownership, see Maxwell (2004).

In other words, outside researchers are still considered the protagonists of these methodologies.

There are many examples of how the language used to describe these methodologies quietly points to academics as agents. For instance, consider the discussion of social justice: "Underlying community-based research is a fundamental principle: community-based research is grounded in social justice and responsibility" (Rice 2018, 16). The use of the term *responsibility* reveals the intended audience to be noncommunity in origin. Community members conducting research in their own communities have a responsibility to the community not because they have a commitment to social justice but because they a part of the community. They will answer to the community for their research practices, regardless of which methodology they espouse. Consequently, "social justice and responsibility" in community-based research refer to an outside researcher's commitment to social justice and an outside researcher's sense of responsibility to the community with whom they work. Community-based research centers the researcher and is defined by ethical researcher behavior.

In community-*driven* research, community ownership and autonomy are definitional to the methodology. The participation of any defined set of researchers, outside or inside the group, is not necessary for the success of a project. While collaboration is a feature of CDR, this methodology prioritizes autonomy over collaboration. The community has full sovereignty over the research, its presentation, its access, and its longevity. With CDR comes recognition of a community's inherent title to the research and its right to define how, when, and by whom the research can be conducted.

Community-driven and community-based research are not incompatible, and when taken to the fullest extent of trust and mutual respect, community-based and community-driven research can look quite similar in the field. Many collaborative and ethical works have been pursued under the banner of community-based research. However, these two methodologies are not equivalent. Consider the shared tenet of mutual trust and mutual respect: community-based research requires "establishing and maintaining solid, respectful, reciprocal, and trusting working relationships" between individuals or groups in the community and linguists who wish to work with the community (Czaykowska-Higgins 2009, 40). This statement holds true for CDR as well, but if a relationship is not meeting those expectations, CDR recognizes the right and authority of the community to terminate that relationship and deny further researcher access. By centering community agency, CDR applies a decolonial lens to the creation of knowledge in a way that does not appear to be definitional in community-based research. Given that research priorities are ultimately not up to the researcher, CDR creates a space for anticolonial research in which the historically marginalized are empowered to direct the work within their own communities. CDR acknowledges a right of ownership that leads to long-term, community-led successes that are not possible via outsider research. This aspect is extremely important in research involving language revitalization, as the lasting success of the overall revitalization depends on community involvement, not researcher involvement.

CDR solicits and directs academic expertise to create products and outcomes that meet community needs, rather than using academic expertise to create products such as language documentation, grammars, and academic publications. This objective does not exclude the production of technical language materials. If a community finds value in linguistic resources, and if said resources are produced in an accessible and collaborative way, the production of grammars and other linguistic documents can be empowering. However, the research activities required of CDR—and of community-based research—tend to deviate from conventional academic research. Activities may include conducting workshops for community members in language pedagogy, organizing venues for the community to exhibit language successes, collaborating with community scholars to produce and publish materials on other aspects of history and culture, or training community members in language software. As a linguist focused on lexicography, I would not have suspected that leading a dozen eight-year-olds in rambunctious games of Sesostrieku Niku (Sesostrie Says) would be part of my research agenda. However, with CDR, the success of the community's efforts to revitalize the language is irrevocably linked to my own work.

It should be noted that the use of community-driven methodologies does not guarantee the success of a given project. Communities are diverse, and members' needs will conflict at times. Power may not be effectively balanced between community and academic partners, and the pressures of an academic tenure and promotion process that does not value the time commitment or work of CDR will continue to push academics toward extractive research methodologies. Potential problems notwithstanding, the approach of CDR has incredible value: unlike extractive methodologies, community-driven scholarship gives space for decolonized undertakings that empower community members and validate their ways of knowing (Smith 2012); the sustained relationships of community members and academic researchers foster accountability and mutual respect; and communities retain ownership of their projects, ensuring that the work will outlast any one individual researcher.

Definition of Community

Throughout this book, I use the word *community* to refer to the stakeholders in the Tunica language revitalization project. Defining community is difficult, as many scholars point out, because communities are not monolithic; they are complex units with various overlapping subgroups, each with its own goals, needs, and agenda (Rice 2011, Schensul et al. 2015). Communities are also dynamic, and the community that begins a research project may be different from the one that finishes it (Rice 2018). I generally use the term *community* in two ways. *Tunica community* refers to any enrolled member of the Tunica-Biloxi Tribe, and *speaker community* (or, interchangeably, *language community*) refers to any member of the Tunica-Biloxi Tribe who has some knowledge of the Tunica language. The speaker community contains members with a wide range of Tunica language abilities, ranging from recent learners to established Tunica speakers. For the purposes of my discussions on community, there are speakers of Tunica whom I consider to be outside of the speaker community, namely academically affiliated linguists who are working with the Tunica-Biloxi Tribe to support revitalization. These speakers are associated with the TLP at the behest of the Tunica community, and though they are also users of the New Tunica Dictionary, the dictionary was not designed with their specific needs in mind. Hence, *community* is limited in scope in that it refers to Tunica-Biloxi groups and individuals.

The Author's Long-Term Community Involvement

Given the breadth of activities that a researcher may undertake when ascribing to community-driven research, the methodology takes considerable time and energy. Trust and mutual respect between all parties involved is critical for the success of the methodology, and these relationships take time to build. I was fortunate to enter my lexicographic research with a relationship with the Tunica-Biloxi Tribe already in place. The lexicographic analysis contained in these pages benefited extensively from a working relationship with the Tunica-Biloxi Tribe that began long before I set out to create a Tunica dictionary. I worked alongside tribal and nontribal scholars on projects proposed by both groups. From creating neologisms for signage on the reservation to manning a booth at the annual Tunica-Biloxi Pow-Wow, I spent as much time on the relationship-building side of the projects as the linguistic side. Tribal members invited us into their homes; we shared meals and danced intertribal dances together at the annual pow-wow. A sense of trust and mutual respect built up with each successive interaction, so much so that I was eventually asked to be the first non-Tunica master teacher for the annual Tunica-led summer camp.

My long-term relationship with tribal and academic members of KYLY afforded insight into the needs of present and future Tunica language learners, teachers, and community members. The dictionary project progressed with regular input solicited from KYLY. Both tribal and academic members of the TLP were extensive collaborators throughout the dictionary construction, especially during the labor-intensive compilation phase. As the dictionary took a more concrete form, prototype dictionary apps were used by language learners, and feedback was gathered. My ongoing interactions with Tunica learners and KYLY members illuminated extralinguistic needs that could be incorporated into the dictionary project. For example, as is common in languages undergoing revitalization, the language community needed new Tunica words in expanded domains. Western research methodologies would have me, the lexicographer, simply document the words that were created once they were produced by Tunica speakers. However, Tunica language learners were not sufficiently familiar with Tunica grammar to make new words; and the few times they did venture to create new words, they harbored a fear that their creations were "wrong" or "inauthentic." In the realm of community-driven research, it would have been unethical of me to merely gather data and walk away. Instead, I used the dictionary as a springboard for community sessions on the process of making neologisms, a process discussed in detail in chapter 5.

My ongoing relationship with KYLY and Tunica language learners meant that my work with the dictionary was sometimes the impetus for changes to the language itself. For example, semantically ambiguous headwords were brought to the group's attention, resulting in heated discussions over domains that lasted several weeks. The outcomes of such discussions often changed delineations of meaning as originally documented in Tunica (more details on this process are found in chapter 4). Conversely, changes made by KYLY regarding Tunica grammar have repercussions through the language, affecting vocabulary both new and old. All KYLY changes were made in full collaboration with Tunica teachers, and all changes are documented in the New Tunica Dictionary to become a lasting part of the Tunica language. The collaborative input from all stakeholders ensures the utility and accessibility of the New Tunica Dictionary by actual Tunica speakers.

The Need for a New Tunica Dictionary

As previously mentioned, the TLP had access to an older dictionary: Haas's 1953 *Tunica Dictionary*. The Haas dictionary is an incredible scholastic work and offers a complete picture of documented Tunica at that time. Haas incorporated not only Youchigant's speech but also language as recorded by Gatschet and Swanton. In the front matter of the *Tunica Dictionary*, Haas clearly outlines how she dealt with discrepancies between her data, Youchigant's linguistic judgments, and the Gatschet-Swanton vocabulary cards, leaving the reader with no doubt of the massive amount of work she did to get the older sources into a usable state.

However, by 2011, just one year into TLP's work, the 1953 dictionary was thoroughly outdated. The process of revitalization has wrought many changes in the language, and the information in the Haas dictionary continues to become more difficult to reconcile with contemporary Tunica each passing year. The most visually striking difference is the update to Haas's orthography: č, š, and ʔ found in Haas's materials are now ch, sh, and ', respectively: *áškaláhpičɛra* is now *ash-kalahpichɛra*, *níštʔɛ* is now *nisht'ɛ*, and so forth. Diacritical markings indicating stress have also been removed from contemporary Tunica. Another aspect that makes the Haas dictionary difficult to reconcile stems from a differing approach to phonology; contemporary Tunica speakers prefer forms such as *michu sah**kuy**tɛya* and *tuchɛhkatonayi* over Haas's *michu sahtɛya* and *ta'uchɛhkatonayi* (or what she rendered as *míču sáhtɛya* and *táʔučɛhkatónayi*; disparate syllables, added in the first example and subtracted in the second, have been highlighted). The reasons behind these phonological changes are a subject for another publication. But from the lexicographic perspective, these differences jar the user when they cannot find what they were looking for in the dictionary.

Subtler and more difficult to detect are the changes and reevaluations of the grammatical features of contemporary Tunica. For example, lexical gender as outlined in Haas (1940) has been dramatically overhauled by the KYLY. Inanimate nouns have been assigned a default gender (Heaton and Anderson 2017). This move renders the noun-class markings in the old *Tunica Dictionary* obsolete. Their presence in the dictionary clutters the page, and Haas's noun-class markings simply confuse learners and KYLY members alike. In another change, verb classes were reassessed and reassigned. The morphologically identical verb classes of transitive Tishlina verbs and stative inchoative verbs were heavily affected by this process (Heaton 2016). Tishlina verbs (Haas calls them impersonal and transimpersonal verbs) describe states or conditions that happen to someone, dubbed Tishlina by KYLY after the folkloric Stone Witch (Anderson and Maxwell, forthcoming); examples include *ashu* 'to sneeze' or *kɛma* 'to have good luck'. Stative inchoative verbs describe entering a certain state, such as *mahka* 'to fall in love'. However, some verbs could not be neatly placed into one class or the other based on semantics alone. And while the two verb classes are morphologically identical, their designation affects acceptable derivations into other classes. For example, the Tunica word *shuli* 'to warm oneself' was listed by Haas as a Tishlina verb, but that class assignment meant it would be impossible to do that action to someone else; the construction "I am warming up coffee" would not be allowed. Consequently, KYLY changed the verb class of *shuli* to stative, which has a mechanism for transforming into an active transitive verb. As part of revitalization, KYLY methodically examined all instances of transitive Tishlina and stative inchoative verbs listed in Haas's dictionary. In some cases, KYLY opted to change the verb classification. The grammatical standing of these updated verbs needs to be reflected in the dictionary if new speakers are to use them properly.

KYLY and Tunica language learners have also created numerous neologisms since the revitalization project began. Words such as *rinis'aha* 'museum' and *tiratasihu* 'towel' were created for the reservation signage project, *yanalepini* 'conversation, dialogue' and *lutamashu* 'grammar' were created for the textbook, and so forth. Before the new dictionary, these words were scattered across Google documents and classroom worksheets. On a regular basis, a KYLY member would ask questions like, "Didn't someone create a word for 'banana'? Does anyone remember what that was?" and time would be spent searching through documents until it was found. Even more important than the benefit of convenience, the incorporation of neologisms into mainstream Tunica is paramount to the continued expansion of the language. As such these words must be represented in published Tunica materials. Placing these words in the dictionary alongside previously attested Tunica words elevates their status as real Tunica and encourages their proliferation and acceptance.

While the TLP is extremely grateful to Sesostrie Youchigant, Mary R. Haas, and the *Tunica Dictionary*, this 1953 dictionary does not meet the needs of contemporary Tunica speakers. Searching the existing dictionary was time consuming and frustrating even for trained scholars; and once the sought-out information was found, it could not be guaranteed to be accurate in the contemporary context. A new dictionary was needed if learners were going to use the language successfully. Through extensive, ongoing community collaboration and team-inspired linguistic prowess, I set out to make the New Tunica Dictionary a functional and comprehensive lexicographic tool.

Chapter Two

Lexicographic Authority and a Colonial Legacy

"How are you going to do that?" This question is often posed—sometimes force-fully, other times quizzically—when I inform folks that I work with a language revitalization project that is teaching a language of which the last native speaker died in 1948. I have ventured various responses over the last ten years of my involvement with the Tunica Language Project (TLP): a very detailed scholar wrote a grammar in a phonetic alphabet; or audio recordings have been uncovered that give us information about the cadence and phrase patterns of the language. But the answer that has been most effective in quelling any further questions about feasibility is as follows: a dictionary was created in 1953. The sheer relief that passes over outsiders' faces with this answer is practically comical. Until that point, lookers-on are absolutely convinced of the impossibility of the task at hand. But once a dictionary is introduced into the mix, they are willing to consider that maybe, just maybe, the TLP has a chance of success.

I always find this reaction somewhat bemusing, as the 1953 *Tunica Dictionary* is not a particularly useful reference in the context of the current revitalization movement. It uses an orthography that contemporary learners do not understand. It has minimal information for English–Tunica entries. It is entirely incomplete in the grammatical categories assigned to nouns. It is an imperfect reference that documents the Tunica language at a specific point in its history, a time in which the language had undergone rapid and devastating language shift. But the relieved reactions of onlookers provide insight into the profound power of dictionaries in the social imaginary. This outdated dictionary imparts assurance that our language revitalization efforts are real and attainable.

Dictionaries inhabit a pedestal that few other works achieve in U.S. English-speaking society. One measure of this is the ways in which we construct and interact with its physical form. The prototypical dictionary is a printed, weighty, leather-bound tome. The household dictionary of my childhood had alphabetic tabs inset with gold embossing. There is even a dedicated piece of furniture, the dictionary stand, with the explicit function of putting one's dictionary on display for others to peruse and admire.[1] The only other book given similar treatment in contemporary U.S. society is the Bible. To say that the dictionary and the Bible occupy the same authoritative tier—on language and morality—is not hyperbole. Indeed, a punishment for poor behavior at my Catholic elementary school often consisted of copying words from the dictionary, as though the interaction with such a book could show us the error of our ways. The range of authority embodied by a dictionary is remarkable, but it has not been accumulated by accident; instead, dictionaries were steadily positioned as authoritative reference works by a long history of lexicography in the Western world.

While this book focuses on Indigenous-language lexicography, the impact of non-Indigenous, particularly European, lexicography on the import and growth of dictionaries is undeniable. Aspects that make dictionaries empowering to smaller language communities, proving their languages to be legitimate, modern, and sophisticated enough to merit a dictionary, are direct outcomes of a historically colonial approach to language via the dictionary and its imposition on nonconforming, non-European speakers. This chapter examines the evolution of lexicography as a means of uncovering the many facets and functions of dictionaries. With a better understanding of the historical uses of dictionaries, we gain insight into the genre's strengths, limitations, and areas for growth. In preparing the New Tunica Dictionary, I found that examining the history of dictionaries prompted me to ask certain questions: What are the parameters in which one can make a dictionary? What assumptions exist due to lexicography's legacy, and how do they

---

1. An internet search for the phrase "buy dictionary stand" is quite eye-opening. Most dictionary stands cost a few hundred dollars, though some cost much more, including one with satin wood inlay on rosewood, costing a mere $19,100 (Robertson n.d.).

impinge on a community's reimaging of a dictionary's look and feel? Which historical assumptions need to be changed by necessity of the language with which we are working? Which assumptions can be bent and molded to fit the expectations of the language users? In what ways does breaking from the conventional lexicographic mold enhance the language revitalization project, and in what ways does it distract the dictionary user and take away from the goal of having the language used? Knowledge of dictionaries' origins enables us to more effectively leverage dictionaries for revitalization, allowing us to reclaim dictionaries as a means for advancing the knowledge and standing of Indigenous-language communities.

A Brief History of Modern Dictionaries

Historians of lexicography[2] generally identify Samuel Johnson's 1755 *Dictionary of the English Language* to be the first modern English dictionary.[3] It is no coincidence that the publication of Johnson's dictionary comes after the height of European colonialism in the Americas: modern lexicography was irrefutably born of the imperial agenda. This fact was openly acknowledged by lexicographers and grammarians of that time period. Spanish lexicographer Antonio de Nebrija, who created the first Castilian language grammar in 1492, reportedly stated that "language is the perfect instrument of empire" (Rafael [1993] 2001, 23). In the preface to his 1571 Spanish–Nahuatl dictionary, *Vocabulario en lengua castellana y mexicana*, Alonso de Molina wrote:

> Where, given that Christian piety inclines us to benefit these natives both in temporal and in spiritual matters, the lack of language impedes us. And it is no small disadvantage that those who govern and rule them, and put everything in good order and

---

2. This section focuses largely on the lexicographic history of European languages. Due to a lack of comprehensive scholarship on Indigenous-language lexicography, a synopsis of the field would require considerable primary research that is outside of the scope of this book.

3. Other English dictionaries were written before Johnson's; however, their "modernity" is often under scrutiny for features such as very limited scope, inconsistent spelling and alphabetization, or a tendency to list every word as a headword instead of using subsenses (Green 1996, 57–58, 174). For an in-depth history of European lexicography, particularly that of English, see Green (1996).

provide them justice, remedying and fixing the grievances which they receive, do not have mutual understanding, rather that the reason and justice which they have are relinquished to the good or bad intentions of the Nahuatl-speaker or interpreter.

Quoted in translation in Clayton and Campbell 2002, 341

Molina felt that an inability to communicate imperiled the spiritual and legal well-being of Spain's Nahuatl subjects, since the "good order" brought by colonial governors was dependent on Nahuatl interpreters. His dictionary was intended to remedy the situation and bring Indigenous Nahuatl-speaking people into the fold for easier governance and salvation. In other words, the peoples of the New World had been conquered militarily; the job of lexicographers was to ensure their conquest culturally, politically, and spiritually. Dictionaries' role in the imperial agenda was not limited to the New World; British colonial administrators leveraged lexicography to solidify rule in India (Cohn 1996). Belgian colonizers consolidated their power in Congo through the appropriation and dissemination of Swahili, and dictionaries such as Père Delaunay's 1885 *Dictionnaire français-kiswahili* were explicitly deployed to communicate with and control Native populations (Fabian 1986, 13–14).

It could be argued that some colonial lexicographers were genuinely interested in learning about and documenting Indigenous languages for the sake of posterity. Many colonial lexicographers were undoubtably both intellectually curious and well intentioned. However, the colonial processes at work were undeniable, even among the best-intentioned lexicographers; lexicographic projects from the sixteenth century to the early twentieth century were, by their very existence, essential to the fabric of the imperial project.

Control at Home and Abroad Through Lexicography

Contemporaneous with colonial lexicographic projects, the nation-building forces that drove conquest abroad were no less at play in the lexicography seen in Europe. The history of lexicography in Europe details the rise of nationalism and the desire of newly formed governments to assert a coherent identity for their subjects. The legacy of European dictionaries cannot be understated; lexicographic assumptions, social roles, and the assignation of authority were all born of the

European lexicographic tradition and subsequently carry into dictionaries today, regardless of the language that these dictionaries encode.

Prior to the fifteenth century, dictionaries were largely multilingual reference works (Mugglestone 2011, 22). In the precolonial European lexicographic tradition, dictionaries were initially seen as useful only in translating between "high" languages such as Greek and Latin. The reluctance to include vernacular languages in dictionaries indicates dictionaries' elevated standing, an early sign that maintaining the status of the genre took precedence over the production of broadly usable references works. Nevertheless, multilingual dictionaries slowly arose, with vernacular languages included as a means of access to and study of the high languages.

By the mid-sixteenth century, dictionaries were well established as multilingual educational instruments (Mugglestone 2011, 24). Several popular dictionaries, such as John Withal's 1556 *A Short Dictionary for Young Beginners*, were designed by teachers to teach English-speaking children Latin, French, and Greek (Hüllen 1999). The 1574 *An Alvearie or Triple Dictionarie in Englishe, Latin, and French* was written by a language tutor, John Baret, based on his work with students of Latin. He compiled the dictionary for use by his students, but he quickly realized its value and published it for the "publike propagation of the Latin tongue" (Baret 1574, n.p.). Dictionaries from this era were teaching tools and therefore carried a degree of authority as they showed students "the proper way" to use each language. However, these dictionaries explicitly stated that they did not hold all knowledge of the language in question. The title of Baret's book, *Alvearie* 'beehive', was chosen to convey the message that it takes many worker bees to build such a lexicographic monument, and users were encouraged to add their own knowledge of the languages "under their proper Tytles" (Baret 1574, n.p.).[4]

Monolingual dictionaries were incredibly rare until the end of the sixteenth century. They first appeared in Europe under the auspices of various language academies. The objective of language academies was to both standardize and affirm

---

4. Interestingly, two book antiquarians claim to have found Shakespeare's annotated version of Baret's *Alvearie*. They have made high-resolution copies of the dictionary available online for free through the website Shakespeare's Beehive, with free registration. While the claim that this volume is Shakespeare's actual dictionary is in doubt, the dictionary is heavily annotated with new words and expressions and is thus evidence that dictionaries at the time lacked ownership over the language.

the status of their native tongue. Academy-created dictionaries were prescriptivist in nature,[5] tending toward the inclusion of language that was deemed "of
value" or "pure" (Mugglestone 2011, 28–29). In contrast, given that there was no
English-language academy, monolingual English dictionaries of the seventeenth
century generally did not discard words for reasons of linguistic impurity.[6] English
dictionaries maintained an important role as teaching tools, which meant that
loanwords that were deemed difficult or unusual were always included (Green
1996; Mugglestone 2011). Elements of the modern dictionary were present in
seventeenth-century works; example sentences from sources, etymological notes,
and alphabetical order were all innovations of seventeenth-century lexicography
(Green 1996). However, the implementation of these features was patchwork,
varying greatly from dictionary to dictionary. A shift toward a more scientific and
scholarly approach would standardize the format of dictionaries in the coming
centuries.

By the eighteenth century, language academies across Europe had strength-
ened; the Académie Française was founded in 1653, the Real Academia Española
in 1713. The language academies sought to use dictionaries as mechanisms to control language. Dictionaries became normative, dictating correctness, good and bad
usage, and acceptable and unacceptable words. In Britain, several public figures
appealed for an Academy of English, one that would standardize orthography, lay
out proper usage, and compile a national dictionary. Johnson's 1755 *A Dictionary
of the English Language* reflected the nationalist sentiments of his time.[7] In his preface, Johnson expressed dismay with the state of the English language:

When I took the first survey of my undertaking, I found our speech copious without

order, and energetick without rules: wherever I turned my view, there was perplexity

---

5. Prescriptivism entails telling users how the language *should* be used. In contrast,
descriptivism involves recording how the language *is* used. A descriptivist lexicographer
of English would include the words *regardless* and *irregardless* in the dictionary, as both are
widely used by English-language speakers. In contrast, a prescriptivist lexicographer would
only include *regardless*.

6. Robert Cawdrey's 1604 *A Table Alphabeticall of Hard Usual English Wordes* is considered
the first monolingual English dictionary. It contains a scant 3,200 words (Peters 1968).

7. Jonathon Green (1996) makes the argument that the success of Johnson's dictionary
allowed Britain to side step the question of a language academy, as its normative approach
fulfilled many of the reasons for wanting a language academy in the first place.

to be disentangled, and confusion to be regulated; choice was to be made out of boundless variety, without any established principle of selection; adulterations were to be detected, without a settled test of purity; and modes of expression, to be rejected or received, without the suffrages of any writers of classical reputation or acknowledged authority.

Johnson 1755, preface

Johnson's work, in his opinion, was to restore national pride by standardizing linguistic "adulterations" and removing "spots of barbarity impressed so deep in the English language" (Johnson 1755, preface).

The contents of Johnson's dictionary clearly reflect the hierarchy of knowledge agreed on by his contemporaries. Most example sentences come from the King James Bible and Shakespeare. These sources were considered not only linguistically pure but also morally authoritative. Proper language use thus indicated that a person was both well educated and morally upright by Christian moral standards. In Johnson we see a reflection of the larger societal agenda: reify the superiority of Christianity and reinforce the political status quo. An infamous example of his dictionary upholding the political status quo is the disparagement of the Scottish in his definition for *oats*: "A grain, which in England is generally given to horses, but in Scotland supports the people." *A Dictionary of the English Language* was the preeminent English-language dictionary for more than 150 years, and its impact as the foundational English-language dictionary is still seen in contemporary dictionaries (regardless of language) published in the United States.

The early nineteenth century continued the tradition of nationalist and prescriptivist dictionaries, such as Noah Webster's 1828 *American Dictionary of the English Language*, which sought to distinguish American English from the British variety by changing the spellings of words. Words affected include *color* (as opposed to the British *colour*) and *civilization* (vs. *civilisation*). The end of the nineteenth century, however, witnessed a shift toward scholarly or "scientific" dictionaries. Rather than educate users on how to be cultured, moral, and patriotic citizens, English-language dictionaries shifted to focusing on research on the language. Seeking legitimacy for their scholarship, lexicographers argued that their methods must become more scientific. It was not the lexicographers' job to intervene in the language, argued German lexicographer Franz Passow; instead, a lexicographer should strive to create a lexicographic narrative that traces the use of a word through time (Mugglestone 2011). Chronologically ordered citations would allow a word to speak for itself, and a lexicographer could scientifically deduce its meaning from the available evidence. This argument led to the seventy-year compilation of the *New English Dictionary*, published in 1928 and renamed the *Oxford English Dictionary* in 1933 (Oxford English Dictionary n.d.c.).

The embrace of the scientific method was not an innovation on the part of lexicographers. Rather, the shift was reactionary, a reflection of the times. Debates on the legitimacy of knowledge were widespread, and the authority of religiously derived truths was diminishing. A move toward scholarly dictionaries was not a break from the historical lexicographic tradition but a continuation of it. By the late nineteenth century, dictionaries were understood to be the most authoritative resource on a language; they must therefore be compiled with the most authoritative sources of information. The parameters for authoritative sources were expanded, with the *Oxford English Dictionary* recognizing the authority of a wider range of print resources. However, the approach continued to embody many prescriptivist tendencies; for example, certain print sources were still considered more legitimate than others.

At the turn of the twentieth century, the role of dictionaries was firmly established. Intellectual and popular users alike agreed that dictionaries should align with at least one of the following categories: "the dictionary as a guardian of linguistic purity; the dictionary as a repository of society's collective knowledge; the dictionary as guardian of absolute and eternal truth; and of the moral and ideological values of society" (Green 1996, 450). Dictionaries were not created *for users*. As is evidenced in the prefaces and front matter of countless dictionaries into the early twentieth century, dictionaries were created to document and protect the knowledge and/or purity of the English language. Users, insofar as they were considered, were assumed to be scholars or scholars-in-training. The purpose of the dictionary was not to be useful to the general public but to be respected, and while dictionaries were not yet common household objects, those found in homes were markers of status rather than tools to be utilized. The first dictionary to break this pattern was the 1913 *New Standard Unabridged Dictionary of the English Language*, from publisher Funk and Wagnalls. This dictionary pioneered several user-focused methods, including a new headword organization based on what a user might actually want to know if they were approaching the dictionary to learn the meaning of a word: contemporary meaning came first, followed by obsolete or archaic meanings, and finally came etymology, the holy grail of historical lexicography (Green 1996).

Webster's Third New International Dictionary of the English Language (fondly referred to as *W3* in most literature), published in 1961, took Funk and Wagnalls's consideration of users one step further; editor Philip Gove was adamant that a truly legitimate dictionary should observe and document actual language use by all speakers regardless of the speaker's scholarly status. Dictionaries were becoming household objects, thanks to expanding public education, the passage of the GI Bill, and Funk and Wagnalls's lexicographic success; Gove felt that the language in the dictionary should accurately reflect the linguistic practices of those who open it. *W3* was the first truly descriptive dictionary of the English language. Definitions were updated for entries like *leggy*. New senses were added to existing words, such as "shake off (the press)" for the entry *shake*. A plethora of previously omitted headwords were added,[8] including *pinup, beatnik, fringe benefit,* and *den mother*. Labels were removed from dozens of words; for example, *sexy* and *phony* were no longer labeled as slang (Skinner 2012). Example sentences were taken not just from printed sources, but from audio sources of heads of state, such as Eisenhower's remark "soon my conclusions will be finalized," which appeared under the word *finalize* (qtd. in Skinner 2012, 255).

However, Gove's strategy of considering users' needs and the dictionary's utility was not deemed acceptable for a morally upright English dictionary, and many vehemently criticized *W3*. No change received more attention than the headword *ain't*, which—though not a new word for this edition—had a new definition that awkwardly read "used orally in most parts of the U.S. by cultivated speakers" and was no longer labeled "colloquial" (Skinner 2012, 11). The removal of the usage label triggered a flurry of scathing, racially motivated attacks on *W3*.

The *New York Times* ran an article in October 1961 calling the *W3* "permissive" and claiming that is was "casting aside its responsibilities" (qtd. in Green 1996, 451). A *Chicago Times* article wondered how writers would be able to write good English since Webster refused to correct them (Skinner 2012). Some reviewers went beyond the mere properness of English, decrying *W3* as an attack on family

---

8. Several of the included headwords were documented before the publication of *Webster's Second* in 1913. However, they were excluded from *Webster's Second* for reasons of being too informal or too fanciful, as was the case with the word *astronaut*, for example (Skinner 2012, 10).

life and a gateway to immorality (Lynch 2009). The *Detroit Times* published an article by Rev. Richard S. Emrich likening *W3*'s permissiveness to the level of national security, stating, "If a sentry forsakes his post and places an army in danger, the penalty is severe. . . . If a great dictionary forsakes its post as guardian of our language, how can one avoid disappointment?" (qtd. in Preston 2002, 149). Emrich was not alone in his concern for national security. The *Toronto Globe and Mail* commented on *W3*, stating, "Where language is without rules and discipline, there is little understanding, much misunderstanding. How can we convey precise meanings to the Russians, when we cannot convey them to each other?" (qtd. in Skinner 2012, 15). At the height of the Cold War, such a claim that the dictionary could be responsible for the deterioration of relations with Russia was quite bold.

These examples of lexicographic backlash are mentioned to illustrate the powerful hold that dictionaries have on the popular imagination in the United States. Dictionaries' linguistic functions are often secondary to their social and moral functions, and information about the language is permitted in a dictionary insofar as it advances the latter. Today, the increasing speed of information exchange has advanced some of the "permissive" tendencies that began with *W3*, especially when it comes to adding new words to the dictionary. However, a view of the dictionary as protector and arbiter of legitimate English language is still prevalent. The weight carried by dictionaries has a profound impact on the usefulness and role of dictionaries in Native American language revitalization, especially in a U.S. context.

Lexicography: The Study of the Making of Dictionaries

While the making of dictionaries was undertaken as far back as 2000 BCE,[9] there are no mentions of manuals or instructions on how to make a dictionary until the twentieth century. Despite the lack of published best practices, every lexicographer seemed to know how they were made, so pervasive was the European model of dictionary formatting. Indeed, the word *lexicography* was documented as early

---

9. The first dictionary on record is of Sumerian and Akkadian, organized thematically and documented in cuneiform on stone tablets (Green 1996).

as 1680 CE,[10] yet the theoretical and analytical study of dictionaries itself is still in its infancy. Consensus within the field hails Ladislav Zgusta's 1971 *Manual of Lexicography* as the first published material to codify how one should approach lexicography as a field. The first question Zgusta tackled was that of what actually defines a dictionary. Zgusta's (1971, 17) definition of a dictionary emphasizes the systematic ordering of community-accepted forms and their meanings. Swedish lexicographer Bo Svensén (1993) later modified the definition of dictionaries to include their use as reference tools that a user consults to determine meaning, verify spelling, or fill a gap in their knowledge. Svensén (2009, 3) broadly divides the field of lexicography into two subfields: the act of compiling dictionaries, also known as practical lexicography, and the study of dictionary compilation, use, features, and history, dubbed theoretical lexicography.[11]

Lexicography Across All Mediums

Subsequent chapters will dive into the tenets that underpin both practical and theoretical lexicography, from dictionary formatting to corpus selection to lexicographic goal orientation. Before turning to such topics, however, I would like to explicitly mention the contribution of technology to the evolution of the dictionary. Until the 1990s, it was rightfully assumed that a dictionary would be printed on paper, and practical lexicographers often used analytical tools eclectically, depending on physical space constraints. Many lexicographers placed their hope in electronic dictionaries as a means of breaking down barriers and traditions maintained by print dictionaries. Early published electronic dictionaries took form on CD-ROM, with the "best known" early CD-ROM dictionary being the *Oxford English Dictionary on Compact Disc*, which was published as a two-disc set in 1987 (Schryver 2003, 190). The CD-ROM was hailed as a boon to lexicography as it mitigated the space constraints that haunted print dictionaries (Leech and Nesi 1999). Lexicographers dreamt of using this newfound space to create

---

10. *Oxford English Dictionary*, s.v. "lexicography," accessed June 6, 2020, http://www.oed .com/.

11. Henning Bergenholtz and Rufus H. Gouws (2012) offer a detailed review of many definitions of lexicography, pointing out the strengths and shortcomings of each. Svensén's definition is generally accepted as adequate.

multilingual "hypertexts" in which the dictionary user could jump from entry to entry with ease (Atkins 1996, 544). However, beyond mitigating space limitations, this technology did not result in any long-term lexicographic innovations.[12]

The advent of the Internet raised hopes of incredible dictionary innovations that could arise, including reinterpretation of dictionary copyright, dictionary search engineering, and collaborative editing (Carr 1997). However, the revolution that technology was supposedly going to bring has yet to unfold. Reputable online dictionaries are simply Internet versions of their print counterparts. There is even evidence that print-turned-digital dictionaries are directly copied from the printed page (Anderson 2017). This is not to say that the Internet hasn't inspired innovations in lexicography. Several attempts have been made to break the mold of conventional top-down dictionary making. Wiktionary.com, for example, allows users to upload definitions for editorial review, and UrbanDictionary.com allows any user to vote on the validity of a definition, completely bypassing established editorial boards. However, these sites do not have the same authority as sites associated with "big" dictionary names, such as Merriam-Webster.com.

The dearth of innovation has led some scholars to argue that theoretical lexicography has no influence over practical lexicography (Bergenholtz 2011), although some theoretical lexicographers are calling for new approaches. The advent of computational linguistics and Internet-based dictionaries has prompted some lexicographers to argue that a new, medium-independent theory is needed. Rufus H. Gouws (2011, 28–29) implores lexicographers to ditch "lexicographic colonialism" and move toward "lexicographic democratization."[13]

It is here that theoretical lexicographers have much to learn from Indigenous-language dictionary making. Indeed, one could argue that lexicographic theory grappling with non-European languages is precisely what has pushed the theoretical field to this point. Indigenous-language lexicographers have long been breaking barriers imposed by the constraints of Western lexicography. Indigenous-language lexicographers have found that weddedness to Western dictionary assumptions

---

12. One can make the argument that CD-ROM did not really do much to solve the space issue either. A multi-disc dictionary set that requires a user to eject one CD and insert another in order to look up a cross-referenced term is just as cumbersome (if not more so) than a print volume that requires users to flip from entry to entry.

13. For further discussion on the distinct lack of innovation, see Tarp (2012); Fuertes-Olivera and Bergenholtz (2011).

results in complications such as arbitrary and confusing headwords (Munro 2002; Pulte and Feeling 2002). Indigenous-language dictionaries produced by twentieth-century scholars pushed the boundaries of lexicography by including grammatical categories not found in earlier iterations, such as alienable and inalienable nouns, language-specific pronominal categories, and animacy classes (Bartholomew and Schoenhals 1983).

That said, the legacy of dictionaries as authoritative objects still influences dictionary construction, regardless of language. The monolith that is the monolingual Western European–language dictionary is deeply ingrained in the psyche of many speakers of American English, and the Tunica community is no exception. With the New Tunica Dictionary, the issue of conforming to lexicographic norms reared its head as a series of questions for the group. Should any word be excluded from the dictionary for any reason? Do we label neologisms or obsolete words in any special way? How do we balance guiding users to create understandable Tunica while also supporting the creativity of language expression? Where our group landed on these issues will be discussed at length in the remaining chapters of this book, which spotlight the linguistic and sociolinguistic functions of the New Tunica Dictionary. It took much work and reimagining, looking at countless sources and example dictionaries, to break away from the monolingual majority-language mold in creating our Tunica dictionary.

Chapter Three
Planning a Functional Dictionary

What is a dictionary meant to do? That may seem like a straightforward question with a straightforward answer: look up a word and discover a meaning. But as we saw in the last chapter, dictionaries have been deployed to accomplish a wide range of things: subjugate peoples, instill a sense of nationhood, teach Latin, document a word's history, help folks understand a word's meaning, enforce normative spelling, and even regulate vocabulary in the service of international diplomacy. In the case of the New Tunica Dictionary, the answer was both obvious and complex: advance the goals of the overall language revitalization project. This objective is quite broad, and the Tunica dictionary team dedicated time and resources to determining how best to achieve it. Our findings informed how we planned and executed the New Tunica Dictionary.

The process of clarifying our goals was one of regular and direct consultation with Tunica community members, with the support and collaboration of the tribally run Language and Culture Revitalization Program. The larger Tunica working group (Kuhpani Yoyani Luhchi Yoroni, KYLY) met twice weekly while the dictionary was being compiled. This time was dedicated to a variety of Tunica language projects, from grammatical findings and clarifications to classroom planning. Dictionary-related topics would arise, the specifics of which are the subject of the next chapter. But the dictionary was not the primary topic of discussion. Rather, these meetings allowed me to keep in step with the evolving needs of the revitalization project. When possible, I sought to align dictionary tasks with revitalization needs. For example, the group needed Mary R. Haas's *Tunica Texts* (1950) to be in a searchable format, a need that aligned with the Tunica dictionary's need for example sentences from historical sources. I therefore leveraged the dictionary to accomplish the larger task. My dictionary team transcribed the texts, KYLY vetted and edited them to adhere to modern Tunica conventions, and I then used the edited texts for example sentences in the dictionary.

My regular attendance at KYLY meetings also anchored the dictionary project to the evolving needs of the various users that the dictionary was meant to serve. Undoubtably, attempting to accommodate a broad dictionary user base entails a degree of difficulty in execution, given that such lexicographic undertakings have a wide range of stakeholders. Groups planning to use the New Tunica Dictionary include Tunica language instructors, Tunica language students, Tunica community members, noncommunity Tunica learners, the non-Tunica research community, and the non-Tunica local community. Each faction may turn to the dictionary for different reasons in hopes of gaining different insights. Integrating these various users into dictionary planning was one of my primary tasks as lexicographer. I found the framework espoused by functional lexicography to be particularly helpful in clarifying specific ways in which that could be accomplished.

Functional Lexicography

The idea that a dictionary has users is not new; indeed, what good is a dictionary if no one uses it? However, the explicit study of who the users are and how and why they use dictionaries is a recent development. Functional lexicography, a term coined by Danish lexicographers Henning Bergenholtz and Sven Tarp (2003; see also Tarp 2000, 2008), focuses on the experience of the dictionary user as evidence for changes to be made to the dictionary structure. It seeks to systematically pinpoint efficacious lexicographic practices by surveying and studying the behavior of actual dictionary users. Dictionary-use surveys ask users about such topics as frequency of dictionary use and the sort of information sought (meaning, examples, collocations, etc.) (Bergenholtz, Bothma, and Gouws 2011; Ulrich 2011). Other metrics include: rate of lookup "success" (i.e., users found what they were looking for) (Dziemianko 2010, Ulrich 2011); amount of time needed to complete a lookup (Bergenholtz 2011); the types of resources that are cross-referenced when performing a lookup (Frankenberg-Garcia 2005); the point at which a user aborts a lookup (Al-Ajim 2002); and the long-term retention of a word when looked up in dictionaries of varying formats (Lew and Doroszewska 2009; Dziemianko 2010).

Proponents of functional lexicography are intent on producing new kinds of dictionaries that are conducive to the expressed goals of users as opposed to the expressed goals of lexicographers. Functional lexicographic research has resulted in several innovative dictionary formats. For example, Henning Bergenholtz and Esben Bjærge created a Danish-Afrikaans database of idioms and expressions that supports four separate dictionaries, with an online user interface that displays them as one product (Bergenholtz 2011). When a user logs into the website, she is asked to select one of the following statements: (1) I read the text, but do not understand the meaning of a fixed expression; (2) I am writing a text with a specific fixed expression; (3) I am writing a text and am looking for a fixed expression with a specific meaning; or (4) I want to know as much as possible about a fixed expression. The statement selected determines which dictionary the user accesses, which consequently affects the kinds of searches performed on the database and the order and amount of information a user sees. If the user selects statement 1, she will be given only the translated gloss of the phrase, whereas if she selects statement 3, she will receive multiple phrases and glosses that cover a range of related meanings. These definitions have more context and example sentences to help the user determine which idiomatic phrase most appropriately conveys the translation. The fourth option includes even more data, such as phrase origins and common collocations. The division of these user needs into different dictionaries ensures that users access the knowledge they need without having to wade through extraneous information that may possibly confuse their situation.

This model quantifies and codifies the reality that different tasks drive users to a dictionary, and that the successful completion of these tasks requires different information. The dictionaries produced by Bergenholtz and Bjærge openly recognize that some information is more helpful when engaging in active language production as opposed to passive language activities such as understanding written or spoken text. The New Tunica Dictionary deployed this asymmetrical technique in its approach to the two sides of the dictionary, Tunica–English and English–Tunica.

Reception Versus Production in Tunica Dictionaries

While often packaged as a single resource, bilingual dictionaries are, in reality, two separate dictionaries that have been stuck together. The bidirectional halves (from Language A to Language B, and vice versa) constitute their own lexicographic works. While a dictionary could contain the exact same information on both sides, real-world dictionaries are rarely executed as such. Instead, one side is favored with more information over the other, depending on the lexicographer's vision of dictionary use. The lexicographer must consider whether the dictionary will be primarily used for language production (such as speaking or writing) or for reception (comprehending existing texts or another speaker).

The overall goal of Haas's *Tunica Dictionary* (1953) becomes immediately clear when the two halves of the dictionary are compared. This dictionary heavily favors the Tunica–English side, which is filled with long entries that include headword, part of speech, source, definition or gloss, etymology, and reference to the *Tunica Texts* (Haas 1950; indicated as TT) or Tunica grammar (Haas 1940; TG). Some entries also include copious cultural or linguistic detail, as well as reference to the Gatschet-Swanton vocabulary cards (G-S) or Sesostrie Youchigant (Y). Entries stemming from the same root are nested below the main headword, giving the user a chance to see the entry in many contexts and forms.

> yáhpu tr. G-S to poison. . . . This term is equivalent to yáhku used by Y. In
>   G-S there is also a var. agent. táyahku.
>   táyahpu (agent.) "poisoner" in ʔúwatáyahpu vine sp.
> yáka intr. to arrive coming; to come, come up, come back
>   yáka + ču (or ču + yáka) intr. to bring; tr. to bring to . . . (TG 5.233)
> yáka- heron, egret; used only in
>   yákaméli c. black heron (clq. "big Joe"), perh. Louisiana heron, Hydra-
>   nassa tricolor ruficollis
>   yákarɔwa c. American egret, Herodia egretta: "white egret"
>   Note: The Tunica did not kill the American egret (TT 35A:f).
>   They believed that if one ate this bird, one could be eating one's
>   ancestors.
>   yákaʔɔšta c. little blue heron, prob. Florida caerulea: "blue egret" (Fr.
>   egret bleu)

In contrast, the English–Tunica side largely contains single-word Tunica glosses, as well as the label ". . c." on select entries to indicate that the verb is Class II.[1] No other information is given, aside from the occasional parenthetical question mark to indicate a questionable equivalence. Unlike the Tunica–English side, this side of the dictionary is formatted in two columns.

heron, big gray wátoruhki	however hínahkuškan
heron, black yákaméli	howl, to héri
heron, black-crowed night kósulétu	huckleberry (?) ríhkušíhtika
heron, great blue kósulétu	hug, to méru
heron, little blue yáka?ɔšta	huge hɛnt?ɛ
hickory rú	human being ?óni
hickory, red rúmili	hummingbird tɛnakɔlakúwatóhku
hickory, white rúrɔwa	hump over, to ha-. . sóhtu
hickory stick rúkɔsa	hundred pólun
hide táhkiši	hungry, to be -yáhpa
hide, to píhu. . c.	hunt, to wɛra. . c.
hide oneself, to píhu	hurricane húraka

The Tunica–English side spans 103 pages, while the English–Tunica side covers only twenty-four. Even though the English–Tunica entries are arranged in two columns, reducing the number of pages for that side, this discrepancy in length reveals the much greater information covered in the Tunica–English side.

This stark contrast indicates that Haas's *Tunica Dictionary* was clearly intended for passive language activities, specifically translating the *Tunica Texts* (Haas 1950). Haas makes clear that there were no speakers of Tunica at the time of her writing, nor were there expected to be new speakers. Production of Tunica would not be a priority for users of the *Tunica Dictionary*. Haas assumed that anyone

---

1. Class II verbs are distinguished from the more common Class I verbs by their endings. Haas felt that these verbs denoted "causative" actions (as in "I cause the tree to fall" or "I felled the tree"), hence her abbreviation. While many verbs in this class do encode causality, many others—such as the verb *rahi* 'to thunder'—do not. KYLY noticed that when learners were told to think of these verbs as causative, they would incorrectly categorize many verbs. Therefore, KYLY ditched Haas's term and renamed the verb Classes I and II. Tunica learners are now taught to memorize the handful of verbs in Class II to determine verb ending.

accessing her dictionary would be doing so with the intent of understanding written Tunica, rather than producing Tunica. Her decision, then, to include copious information on the Tunica–English side makes sense. Tunica would be the point of entry for users reading her texts. While useful for passive language activities, the Haas dictionary is unreliable when it comes to producing Tunica. The English–Tunica side does not have enough information to result in correct usage. Consequently, accuracy is only achieved when a user performs a "double lookup," finding the word in the English–Tunica index, and then searching for the Tunica word on the Tunica–English side. The double lookup results in a complete picture of the word.

In my experience with the Tunica revitalization project, the double lookup is too arduous for users to do regularly. Lacking complete grammatical and semantic information, the Haas dictionary often leads to incorrect and confusing usage of Tunica. For example, a KYLY group member attempted to construct a Tunica sentence using the word for *to throw*, as in "The child threw down his blanket and stormed out of the room." An examination of the English–Tunica side suggests that the clear verb choice would be *waka* 'to throw it down', a Class II verb (emphasis added).

> throw, to wíya; tóhu
> throw (a liquid) on, to hɛša. . c.
> throw (a liquid) out, to léhki
> throw into (a liquid), to tóhu
> **throw it down, to wáka. . c.**
> throw (over the shoulders), to sáhi, sáhi. . c.
> throw up (vomit), to léhu; rúhu

However, a search for *waka* on the Tunica–English side reveals that *waka* is semantically aligned with "to fell a tree." The Class II properties of the verb support the "fell" sense:

> wáka intr. to fall, topple over (esp. of a tree)
> wáka adj. fallen (of a tree)
> wáka. . c. tr. to fell . . . (a tree); **to throw . . . down**

In fact, *wiya* or *tohu* is probably the best choice here, and these verbs include a gloss "to throw down" in the Tunica–English definitions that is missing from the English–Tunica side.

> tóhu tr. to throw . . . down; to throw . . . away, discard . . . ; to throw . . . (in
>   a liquid)
> wíya tr. to throw, throw down, throw away, throw off . . .

The fact that the 1953 *Tunica Dictionary* was not designed to facilitate Tunica production is extremely problematic for Tunica revitalization; the necessity of double lookups described above is enough to disqualify Haas's dictionary as a useful resource for today's Tunica learners. Before we had even drafted a single entry, KYLY decided that the New Tunica Dictionary should be primarily focused on production, with receptive activities being supported insofar as doing so did not impede productive activities. And so, the balance of information is transposed, with more information on the English–Tunica side of the dictionary. This does not mean that we ruled out reception. We still fully expect users to consult the New Tunica Dictionary for translation of the Haas texts and other Tunica they encounter in the world. Fortunately for us, the advent of digital dictionaries meant that we would not have to sacrifice information useful for reception on the Tunica–English side of the dictionary for the sake of space. From the outset, the Tunica Language Project (TLP) stated that it would like the dictionary to be available in digital form as well as the traditional print form. With this objective in mind, I set out to determine what tool would be best for compilation and storage of the Tunica lexicon.

Functional Dictionary Software

Gone are the days of meticulously gathering thousands of paper dictionary slips for editing and organizing a new dictionary. We have arrived in an age where we have many options for digital compilation and storage of lexicographic data. In fact, there are so many options, that it is somewhat of a head scratcher in figuring out what to use. While preparing the New Tunica Dictionary, I reached out to nearly a dozen seasoned experts who had worked on community language dictionaries for their advice. The software they use spans the gamut of available options, from everyday software such as text editors to complex databases of their own construction. Several made a deliberate choice in their software; others fell into a software out of necessity or precedent. Each had their own reasons for the software they used, and they all talked about the benefits and drawbacks of their decisions. I outline here the software considerations made for the New Tunica Dictionary. I am not affiliated with any of the developers or products mentioned, and I do not intend our process be a mandate for a "best" approach to selecting lexicographic software. However, I hope that this section is useful to anyone attempting to navigate this part of the dictionary-planning process, as it was the source of more than one headache endured by the Tunica dictionary team.

The medium in which the dictionary will be distributed (print, digital, or both) is a key consideration when choosing the software used to compile it. Some software packages make digital or print publication easier than do others. A common go-to for smaller dictionary compilation is a word processor such as Microsoft Word; this style of tool is useful in that it allows dictionary authors to simultaneously record and format the data to be presented. Word processors are also fairly user friendly and familiar to contributors, particularly those who may not be as familiar with newer technologies. In the case of Tunica, two new lexicographic items had been created with Microsoft Word in the past decade: bilingual glossaries that accompanied the children's stories of *Hichut'una Awachihk'unanahch (Fighting Eagles)* and *Tayak Takohkuman (Deer and Turtle)* (Tunica-Tulane Working Group 2011). Microsoft Word and other word processors have been used in making other dictionaries, such as those for Vanuatu (Thieberger 2011) and Nez Perce (Aoki 1994). Lexicographic items produced in word processors are a step up from those that are handwritten; and if self-publishing, even someone with only rudimentary technical skills can use a word processor to produce a highly stylized, visually appealing print dictionary.

However, word processors have some considerable drawbacks. First, they will necessarily be in print form only; there is no easy way to convert a Word document into a website or a web-based dictionary. And while seeing print-ready formatting on screen is a benefit of this tool, formatting can be tedious and frustrating as greater numbers of entries are gathered. Modern word processors now offer a wider variety of automated formatting tools, but they still rely heavily on manual formatting edits. The most serious drawback of using text editors is the single-use aspect of the data: word processors trap data in static, unusable data structures.[2] The data will need to be manually retyped, reformatted, and so on if it is to be used in future projects. This constraint is not ideal for communities with limited resources. Creating a dictionary is a substantial investment, with an incredible amount of time and effort spent selecting and updating data to acceptable community standards. If a word processor is used to compile the dictionary, the process of reusing this community-approved product to create other resources (such as phrase books, semantic dictionaries, and thesauruses) will require additional, substantial effort.

In lieu of word processors, databases with carefully planned data structures provide flexibility for language research and future iterations of the dictionary. Lexemes stored in a database can be reused or outputted to different formats, with the same data easily transformed into a dictionary, story glossary, or a handbook of useful phrases. Theo J. D. Bothma (2011) suggests that finely tuned data could allow an electronic dictionary to display different lexicographic information to users based on their needs. One could account not only for the question of production versus reception but also for other criteria such as language experience, user age, and user interest in the modern spoken language or older, written forms. With such a filter in place, dictionary users could be shown different lexicographic information based on their criteria. In other words, databases are flexible, reusable investments that allow quick reorganization and export of data based on the needs of community members.

Using a database to store a wide variety of data points also makes the data usable for nonlexicographic analysis (Thieberger 2011), benefiting future language research. I need the data for the dictionary, but who knows what language learners, teachers, and researchers will need in the generations to come? In addition to standard dictionary fields such as word, part of speech, and definition, databases can be designed to hold information such as which words are neologisms, the full source of the word including page number, and word correspondences in every analyzed text; this information is useful to linguists and language workers advancing their understanding of the language. For example, one can easily ask, "which texts reference this word?" or "how has the meaning of this word changed

---

2. Nick Thieberger ([1995] 2005, 2011) discusses this problem quite extensively.

during revitalization?" Including this kind of information in a print dictionary may not be appropriate, and the excess would clutter the page, making it virtually unusable for the average user. A database allows all information to be stored without visually surfacing all of it in the final dictionary project, seamlessly meeting the needs of both language learners and language researchers. This versatility is only possible with well-structured data storage.

There are two options that enable this level of flexibility: out-of-the-box lexicographic software specifically designed for dictionary work or a customized in-house database. Choices in prefab lexicographic software for minority languages are limited, especially if one wants to build a dictionary informed by a corpus (a compilation of texts that show real-world language use; it is a lexicographic tool that I discuss at length in the next section). I initially considered lexicographic tools designed for any language, but I quickly found that they were prohibitive due to a high cost or a lack of minority-language features such as Unicode character support or customizable parts of speech labeling. I then focused on software that was solely designed for minority-language use. Many such programs are free for communities working on their language. In the end, only two options were considered potentially viable for our project: Fieldworks Language Explorer (FLEx) and Miromaa.[3]

FLEx is published and maintained by SIL International, formerly known as the Summer Institute of Linguistics.[4] SIL is a Christian missionary organization with the explicit mission "to apply language expertise that advances meaningful development, education, and engagement with Scripture" (SIL n.d.). FLEx is a robust software package, intended to facilitate a wide range of language-collection activities such as gathering stories, eliciting word lists, and recording linguistic variation between speakers or communities. In addition to dictionary creation, FLEx supports several nonlexicographic components such as an interlinear analysis section, a grammar section, and even a parser to speed up the analysis of future texts. Analyzed sentences in the inputted texts can be extracted for use in dictionary entries with the click of a button. The dictionary can be organized alphabet-

---

3. Technology is ever shifting. I base my discussion here on the programs as they existed at the time of writing.

4. As of 2020, the organization is still registered with the IRS as Summer Institute of Linguistics Inc (EIN 75-1840827); however, its website clearly states that it has rebranded and now goes by SIL International (SIL n.d.).

ically or thematically, and FLEx supports multiuser edits to the same database via a networked connection or SIL's LIFT Bridge, which allows users to see and edit data from any location. Collaboration by users in different geographic locations was crucial to our project and not a problem easily solved by most dictionary software (Hatton 2011), so this feature was key for our purposes.

However, the robustness of the FLEx software is one of its most significant drawbacks. FLEx was designed for technically trained field linguists. The sheer number of available database fields is daunting. On a single sense of a word, one can record notes about phonology, grammar, and semantics, as well as bibliographic information, source, scientific name, encyclopedia information, restrictions, usages, complex forms, variants, subentries, and much, much more. These fields are key to a field linguist or trained lexicographer, but FLEx is intimidating to nonacademic language experts. It is not ideal for community members' daily use. What's more, FLEx's organization and data flow are not always intuitive, making it difficult for less technology-savvy users to use, linguistically trained or not. Given the collaborative nature of our work, these challenges were problematic.

Yet, the most egregious drawback of FLEx is its data structure. FLEx uses a proprietary object-oriented database. This innovation means that extracting and reusing data in a non-FLEx interface is technologically intensive. One can create a custom connection to the database directly using a third-party connector, FLExTools (Farrow 2019), but this program can be time consuming and requires a high level of computer programming skill. An alternative method to extracting data from FLEx for publication is to use the built-in XML (Extensible Markup Language) export feature. The exported XML is clunky and requires considerable investment of time and resources to decode and transform into a usable data object that can then be transposed to a website or a printed style sheet. Many revitalization groups working with FLEx have decried this aspect of the program. The lack of a clean export mechanism sheds light on the fact that the original intention of FLEx was to extract linguistic data out of language communities with little plan to reinvest the raw data in the language community.[5]

Regardless of FLEx's original intent, it has a robust community of users and developers who are committed to making the software work for diverse needs,

---

5. For more on the prepackaged colonial assumptions of language software, see Turin (2016).

especially for groups who are actively working in language revitalization. FLEx has an active Google group, where users can field questions to be answered by SIL staff and advanced FLEx users, usually in under twenty-four hours. Members of the FLEx development team take feature requests seriously. One language activist shared that her project needed data that was in FLEx but not in the standard XML export. FLEx developers created a custom export for her team within days. The SIL team has also invested resources in creating a variety of apps to natively consume FLEx's unwieldly XML export so that users do not need to manipulate the raw data themselves. One such example is Pathway, which outputs the data in print-dictionary format.

However, FLEx's technical barriers and the necessity for regular interaction with software developers are not ideal for software that will be used by nontechnical community members and language activists participating in a dictionary project. Miromaa, whose name means "saved" in the Awabakal language, was developed to address the shortcomings of FLEx.[6] Miromaa dictionary software was developed by the Miromaa Aboriginal Language and Technology Centre; in other words, it was designed by Indigenous-language activists for Indigenous-language activists. Initially designed for Aboriginal Australian languages, this software is now used by more than 150 Indigenous-language groups around the world (Miromaa n.d.a.).

One feature that facilitates usability involves giving users different screens based on their role within the project. Users can be designated as a linguist, learner, or community editor. A linguist user sees more data fields for editing than does a community user, who can edit headword, gloss, and multimedia fields. In addition to the user-specific screens, Miromaa supports various user permissions to different areas of the lexicon, allowing the administrator to set multiple levels of editing. These user-specific features are a big draw for the program when many contributors are involved. Miromaa also allows the attachment of audio and written source files to a dictionary entry, a feature that appealed to the Tunica project. Miromaa regularly adds features, including recently support for the creation of an iOS app, though project staff must send Miromaa the language data for its tech experts to build the app. Finally, the program sits on a standard SQL (Structured

---

6. Miromaa's (n.d.b.) informational pamphlet calls out the ways in which it is designed to surpass FLEx in its usability.

Query Language) database, making the information easily extracted for other uses, such as website building.

Miromaa supports multiple users contributing to the same dictionary, but only if their computers are networked. Sharing the data outside of a networked environment requires the exchange of a physical USB drive passed from person to person.[7] This feature is by design, as the software is primarily intended for use in Indigenous-run language centers. I worked directly with Miromaa creator Daryn McKenny to see whether we could overcome this limitation, but in 2014, when work on the Tunica dictionary began, we could not find a feasible workaround for the geographically diffuse Tunica group. Unfortunately, the inability to collaborate over different networks rendered Miromaa unusable for the Tunica project.

A final option for lexicographic data storage is creating one's own proprietary database to house the dictionary data. This option gives the most flexibility, allowing lexicographers to tailor the entry fields to their exact language needs. User-friendly interfaces can be created to allow nontechnical users to navigate and edit the data. Data is imported uniformly, making it easy to export and reformat in a myriad of ways. The Yurok Dictionary Project (Garrett 2011) is a good example of a large-scale, multimedia project that uses such a database. In 2013, Tulane graduate student Amy Peterson created a proof-of-concept Access database for the Tunica dictionary project. This option was appealing in that we had full control over every aspect of data mapping. But full control is a double-edged sword. The drawback to this system is the level of technical expertise a community must have in order to build and maintain it. Even if expertise is available, time spent maintaining a database after its creation is time not spent working on the language.

So rather than reinvent the wheel, I choose FLEx as our dictionary software, despite initial misgivings. The highly active community of users and developers means that FLEx will likely be supported and improved far into the future. The size of the FLEx user community means that new technologies in minority-language lexicography are likely to have FLEx support. For example, a dictionary app maker was published in March 2016 that only supports data in FLEx XML

---

7. Miromaa now supports a robust import/export feature, which could be viable for smaller, geographically diffuse groups working on a dictionary together. However, there is no accounting for merging data changes made by two users at the same time, so work can be easily overwritten if the group does not *carefully* manage workflow. This feature was not available at the time of my initial software assessment.

format. Ultimately, the size of the FLEx community and the ability to collaborate with users in different geographic regions via FLEx's LIFT Bridge were the deciding factors in software choice.

Since inputting the Tunica lexicon and texts into FLEx, the TLP has used the information to answer a variety of questions. Sample questions we have since been able to answer using the FLEx database and its exported XML files include:

What words relate to weather?

How many Tishlina verbs are there?

How many words are based on stems for various body parts? What frequency of these words refer to clothing?

How many disyllabic words exist in Tunica?

How many words end with /ɛ/ or /ɔ/? How many of that subset are monosyllabic?

What is the ratio of voiced to unvoiced consonants in the Tunica lexicon?

The final example was asked by the creators of Rohina Luwa, the Scrabble GO–style game seen in this book's first chapter. The game makers used the data regarding distribution of letters to determine which consonants they needed more of in their card deck.

We have encountered some limitations due to our choice in software, and on more than one occasion the nonintuitive nature of FLEx has caused a confused team member to delete or corrupt large swaths of data. I regularly back up the FLEx database to prevent such loss. FLEx does not give administrators a way to limit certain users' ability to overwrite the database, so I vigilantly check new additions to the database and restore data when needed. Fortunately, a full restore does not happen often. This limitation has been discussed with FLEx's developers, and solutions offered include relegating the problematic user to a nonlinked FLEx database so they can access the data but not touch the master database. However, this solution would not work for a group as active as ours, in which team members are updating FLEx data on a weekly basis. On the other hand, our selection in dictionary software unwittingly gave the Tunica dictionary team opportunities we did not anticipate. For instance, when the TLP decided to rename the verb class previously known as personificatives as Tahch'i Rahihta, we were able to easily use FLEx's custom part-of-speech categories to update all entries of that type; abbreviations and entry formatting were dealt with automatically by FLEx. Additionally, the inputting of texts alongside our lexicon provided the TLP with access to a corpus and allowed the dictionary team to entertain the possibility of corpus-based lexicography. Overall, we are happy with the flexibility FLEx has granted our team.

Corpus Lexicography

Corpus-based lexicography determines the meanings of words based on frequency of word use in published texts. Corpora are assembled sets of texts that, when analyzed, provide evidence of language choices made by language users (Sinclair 2003, 167). For the Tunica dictionary, our corpus was quite small, though growing with each passing year of contemporary language use. The "Texts & Words" area of FLEx made searches for collocations and individual morphemes simple. Collocation refers to the words that commonly appear side by side, such as *open* and *road*, or *heavy* and *sleeper*. Words that frequently appear juxtaposed are of special interest to lexicographers, as these relationships may be important to note in a word's dictionary entry. But in the end, the New Tunica Dictionary did not rely heavily on corpus lexicography, though some limited references to the corpus were used in the construction of example sentences. Still, given its prevalence throughout the lexicographic realm, I feel it worthwhile to briefly discuss corpus lexicography, should another group find it helpful to their situation.

Contemporary corpora are digital, allowing full-text search of their contents. Corpora are used in a wide variety of language research, including natural language processing. Quality corpora include metadata for each text, such as the origin of the text, its authors, its audience, the author-audience relationship, the circumstances of the text, and the medium in which it appeared (Sinclair 2003). Corpora can be designed for evidence of general language use, compiling a wide range of general texts, or they can be field specific, limiting their textual evidence to certain domains. In lexicography, corpora are used to determine meaning and frequency of collocations. Since corpora can compile dozens of sources of naturally occurring language use, corpus-based lexicography is deemed more objective and therefore more authoritative than non-corpus-based lexicography and is considered to be the gold standard of Western dictionary making. Most contemporary dictionaries of world languages center on a corpus, be it a proprietary corpus such as COBUILD or an open-source corpus, such as the Corpus of Contemporary American English.[8]

However, corpus-based lexicography is not without problems: the quality of corpora varies based on their size, their diversity of sources, and the skill of their assemblers. Furthermore, corpora decontextualize examples from their original sources, making it difficult for lexicographers to determine the quality of the examples. Decontextualization compounds any bias found in the sources or in the speakers at large. Lynda Mugglestone (2011) uses the definitions for the senses of *heave* found in the 1987 *Collins COBUILD English Dictionary* as an example of culturally based gender bias passed from corpus to dictionary. *Heave*, meaning "to move something heavy using lots of effort," is accompanied by the following example sentences: "Lee heaved himself with a groan from his chair," "He heaved a table at me," and "'Heave!' cried Jack." In contrast, *heave* as in "something moves up and down or in and out with large regular movements" is exemplified by the sentence "She was in a state of suppressed emotion: heaving breasts and short breaths." In the first sense, masculinity and physical power are interwoven, while femininity and emotional fragility are highlighted in the second. Mugglestone (2011, 111) does not lay the blame solely on the dictionary; COBUILD dictionaries exclusively use unedited example sentences gathered from their corpus.[9] But given the power and authority dictionaries wield, critical self-reflection is crucial for lexicographers. Lexicographers disagree on the extent to which they should interfere with data as given in the corpus. Since corpora decontextualize text, and frequency is the determinative factor of words in corpora, lexicographers must form a policy "concerning the ways in which the corpus will be used; in what ways, if any, it will be supplemented; how any conflicts of expectations and evidence will be resolved" (Sinclair 2003, 167).

---

8. COBUILD is an acronym for the Collins Birmingham University International Language Database. COBUILD advertises itself as "the source of authentic English," and it specifically markets to language learners with a variety of corpus-based resources, including the monolingual *Collins COBUILD English Language Dictionary*, first published in 1987 (COBUILD n.d.). The Corpus of Contemporary American English, or COCA, is maintained by Bingham Young University. It can be accessed here: https://www.english-corpora.org /coca/.

9. For a more critical review of gender bias in the COBUILD dictionaries, see Kaye (1989).

The lexicographers of the New Tunica Dictionary did not have the luxury of deciding to pursue a corpus-based approach, as the Tunica-language corpus is quite small. Other communities have deliberately opted against corpus lexicography due to the quality or source of the texts.[10] The overall reliance on corpora reveals the linguistic privilege that major world languages enjoy, with access to vast quantities of searchable texts deemed unbiased and credible by language speakers. Corpus lexicography can be beneficial in that it balances native-speaker intuition with documented use and places words in a larger use context. However, the amount of time required to gather and organize a corpus along with evaluating the quality or origins of the documentation available may render corpus lexicography inappropriate or untenable for many dictionary projects.

Embracing the Social Role of the Dictionary

Many stakeholders were involved in the Tunica dictionary project, and they all envisioned different tasks to be completed with a functional dictionary. Some of their goals were linguistic in nature, but most were extralinguistic. Tunica teachers wanted to use the dictionary to more easily create lessons and have students engage with the language. Tunica learners wanted to be able to understand the language put in front of them, particularly written language. Tunica tribal members wanted to elevate respect for Tunica and the people who speak it, and as such they were keen to have the Tunica language showcased in a modern, searchable format. Tunica linguists wanted to convey clear use of Tunica grammar in dictionary entries; linguists and linguists-in-training, both tribal and noncommunity, wanted concrete information about the productive forms decided on in the new Tunica grammar, all the better if they could see this information in sentence- or phrase-long contexts. Language researchers wanted analyzable data they could apply to other research projects. As head lexicographer, I wanted users to be excited about using the New Tunica Dictionary, to feel a sense of ownership in the final project. I also wanted to weave dictionary compilation into Tunica student environments.

---

10. Erin Debenport (2015) gives a detailed account of the San Ramón Kiowa language community's decision not to use an existing corpus when constructing its dictionary.

Again, the framework of functional lexicography helped our project understand the ways in which the desires of these stakeholders could be met. In contemporary lexicographic theory, grammatical and linguistic questions are not central driving factors in dictionary creation; instead, functional lexicography focuses solely on the target dictionary user. The expressed, documented desires of the dictionary users drive the planning and execution of the dictionary. The needs expressed by users and subsequently fulfilled by a dictionary can certainly be linguistic; for example, in the case of the New Tunica Dictionary, we want a user to be able to understand Tunica texts as well as create new Tunica phrases. But a core innovation of functional lexicography is the explicit recognition that a dictionary can serve nonlinguistic functions. Functional lexicography moves dictionary compilation away from the linguistic-oriented approach that dominated much twentieth-century lexicography and into what Pedro A. Fuertes-Olivera and Sven Tarp (2011, 142) call "an area of social practice." Under previous lexicographic theories, the examination of the social role of dictionaries—the authority and weight that they have in the popular imagination—was largely ignored. In contrast, by asserting that lexicography is a science of social practice, functional lexicography expressly focuses on "potential users and *the social situation in which they participate*" (Tarp 2008, 40, emphasis added). In other words, the extralinguistic experience of dictionary users should directly inform dictionary creation.

Extralinguistic use of dictionaries will be no surprise to Indigenous-language lexicographers, as scholars have documented a wide range of extralinguistic functions that the planning and implementation of a dictionary can bring about within a language community. For example, dictionaries help standardize a language, particularly if the language is moving from an oral to written medium (Frawley, Hill, and Munro 2002); monolingual dictionaries can create new domains of use (Cablitz 2011); and the process of dictionary compilation can aid in skill transfer and capacity training within a given community (Ogilvie 2011b). In this sense, functional lexicography merely formalizes a process long seen in Indigenous-language lexicography.

Functional lexicographers define "user" as one individual. User needs are specific to that individual or individuals of a similar type (Tarp 2011, 63). However, this theoretical framework opens the door to extending the definition of "user" to encompass an entire speech community. The implications of viewing the community as a dictionary user are profound when applied to languages undergoing revitalization. Functional lexicography challenged me as a lexicographer to ask about the nonlinguistic needs of the Tunica speech community. Working with the Tunica language community, the members of the TLP drafted the following linguistic and extralinguistic goals as objectives of the final Tunica dictionary:

- reinforce a standard orthography
- make Tunica legacy materials accessible to the Tunica language community by using them as sources for example sentences
- codify grammatical categories of contemporary Tunica
- disambiguate meaning of Tunica words found in historical Tunica texts
- expand Tunica into new domains
- encourage learner creativity by soliciting active engagement in the creation of neologisms
- foster community ownership of the language

With those goals in mind, I made concrete decisions about what would and would not be included in the dictionary. I structured dictionary entries in deliberate ways to aid the TLP in reinforcing standard Tunica. I highlighted certain information specific to production of Tunica. I chose definitions for ambiguous terms based on similar words in the language. These decisions were conscientious and deliberate; the changes were also transparent, and I presented each specific change to the larger KYLY. The details of the thought process behind these decisions are the topic of chapters 4 and 5. The specifics of dictionary structure and word representation covered in the next chapter instigated a higher number of intragroup disagreements about how they should be handled. However, the consensus-building foundation that was laid during the dictionary-planning phase assured the various parties that their needs were taken seriously for final considerations in the dictionary.

The meticulous work involved in deciding on lexicographic software, clarifying the importance of production versus reception, and considering the role of existing Tunica texts was crucial in my ability to execute these finite determinations and shaped the outcome of the New Tunica Dictionary. The expectation of ongoing dialogue throughout these comprehensive decisions benefited the next phase of dictionary production. Given the rippling effect of these early decisions,

I highly encourage any group considering a dictionary to pause and examine these aspects before getting too deep into mechanical lexicographic tasks such as headword entry. I will mention that the Tunica dictionary group did some of these "planning" stages after we had already started the dictionary, and it did not impede our progress. Steps that include ongoing dialogue, such as determining the social function of the dictionary, will need to be revisited several times over the course of compilation. Nevertheless, considering the planning aspects outlined in this chapter greatly benefited the New Tunica Dictionary's trajectory and result.

Chapter Four
Making a Dictionary

The act of creating a dictionary is the heart of practical lexicography, a field where theory and planning meet implementation. Practical lexicography has long been undertaken by diverse groups of scholars, language teachers, historians, priests, missionaries, linguists, economists, medical practitioners, and more. The diversity of scholars is reflected in the diversity of topics and approaches to dictionary organization. But regardless of the author, all dictionaries share some basics of structure. Lexicographers divide dictionary structure into three categories: macrostructure, microstructure, and megastructure. Macrostructure refers to the organization of words in a dictionary (Sterkenburg 2003, 6); for example, words in a dictionary could be ordered alphabetically or semantically. Microstructure refers to the information given about each headword. Information pertaining to spelling, pronunciation, part of speech, etymology, lexical meaning, pragmatic usage, collocations, and morphology are all part of the microstructure. Megastructure refers to the larger dictionary structure, including the design of front matter and decisions regarding order of languages in a bilingual dictionary.

As we will see in this chapter, all aspects of dictionary structure, from what constitutes a word to where it lives in the dictionary, are at the discretion of the lexicographer. Many people have preconceptions of what a dictionary should look like, but none of these are absolute mandates. The inclusion or exclusion of structural components is configurable, and the choices made often tell us more about the people making the dictionary than about the language it describes.

The process of making the New Tunica Dictionary was rife with conversations spurred by structural decisions. Concrete structural decisions intersected with larger revitalization ideologies. Should nonstandard Tunica be labeled as such in the dictionary? How should we nudge dictionary users to use contemporary Tunica while still including older, obsolete Tunica forms? Discussions about dictionary structure not only affected the resulting dictionary, but steered decisions of the overall language revitalization project. Lexicographic decisions made by the entire Tunica language working group (Kuhpani Yoyani Luhchi Yoroni, KYLY) encompassed topics such as language authenticity, distinctions of grammar, approaches to pedagogy, and representation of written versus spoken language. These discussions will be interwoven throughout the chapter as I lay out the concrete structural decisions anyone should consider when constructing a dictionary of their own. It is my hope that this chapter is useful to any group undertaking practical lexicography or any individual interested in reimagining dictionary form.

Microstructure: The Dictionary Entry

In its starkest form, a dictionary entry consists of a headword and a definition or gloss. *Definition* is the term used when referring to monolingual entries, while bilingual dictionaries tend toward the term *gloss*. However, the microstructure of a dictionary entry can be as complicated as the lexicographer would like it to be. A dictionary entry can include everything from historical etymologies to illustrations to example sentences. All aspects of the entry itself fall under the category of microstructure.

The microstructure of the two sides of the New Tunica Dictionary is asymmetrical, and the two sides differ in the amount of information they give. As discussed in the last chapter, the Tunica dictionary team had a clear understanding of the dual nature of bilingual dictionaries; the asymmetry in microstructures reflects our expectation that Tunica dictionary users will use each side to different ends. The overall microstructure of the Tunica dictionary entries is as follows:

> **Tunica headword** *part of speech* English gloss: *Tunica example sentence.* English translation. [Extralinguistic information] {*label*}
>
> **English headword** Tunica gloss *Tunica part of speech* {label} [Extralinguistic information] [Grammatical information] *Tunica example sentence.* English translation

As seen here, the English–Tunica entries have a grammatical information component that their Tunica–English counterparts lack. Since the English–Tunica side is used for production, KYLY felt it was important to pack the entries with more information that might lead to correct usage. The inclusion of collocations and full verbal paradigms was also considered, as this information elucidates common language use. Similarly, the label component of the microstructure is earlier in the entry on the English–Tunica side to encourage word selection suitable to the context in which the user is working. A balance between informativity and intelligibility must be carefully struck. Too much information clutters an entry, obscures key information, and may ultimately result in user confusion or language misuse. Print dictionaries are generally more concerned with this balance, if for no other reason than to keep the cost of printing down. However, it has been shown that even in the realm of digital dictionaries, too much information can lead to unsuccessful or frustrating lookups.[1] If a user is presented with an overwhelming amount of information, he most often chooses the first sense of a word without reading the rest of the entry (Tono 1984).

Using this logic, one could argue that one of the most unusable entries in any English dictionary is the entry for the word *set*. The *Oxford English Dictionary* lists nine distinct entries, some with as many as thirty-seven subentries and seven sub-subentries, and the digital content for *set* spans more than 221 pages when printed to pdf.[2] Because *set* is one of the most robust words in the English language, a series of lexicographers decided to divide it into distinct entries and subentries; strategies to inform their decisions may have been based on research, corpus linguistics, native-speaker intuition, or crowdsourcing. While the headwords are a

---

1. Bartosz Ptasznik (2013) gives an excellent overview of landmark dictionary navigation studies to date.

2. *Oxford English Dictionary*, s.v. "set," accessed December 18, 2018, http://www.oed.com.

defining feature of dictionaries, determining headwords is a subjective task. Words that "make the cut" as their own headword as opposed to a subentry of a larger headword are ultimately at the discretion of the lexicographer.

Determining the Headword

The most fundamental component of a dictionary entry is the headword or lemma.[3] However, determining what a headword is or how headwords should be organized in the dictionary is a surprisingly complex task. Complicating factors include derivational forms, the prevalence of suppletive word forms, spelling variation, polysemy, and homonymy. For example, will the dictionary include regularly derived word forms as their own entries? In *Merriam-Webster*,[4] *teach* and *teacher* get separate headwords, but *walk* and *walked* do not. What merits that distinction? What about including irregular or suppletive word forms? In English dictionaries, *taught* and *wrote* get headwords, but regular past-tense conjugations do not. Are spelling variations (e.g., *axe* and *ax*) included as headwords, even if only to redirect users to the more acceptably spelled entry? When are homonyms separated into distinct headwords,[5] and when is one a mere subsense of the other?

Most contemporary majority-language dictionaries borrow the headword determinations from predecessor dictionaries. This practice saves the lexicographer time and builds a lexicographic convention that is familiar to consistent dictionary users. However, this means that any problems present in predecessor dictionaries are carried forward. For example, the notion that the headword should be the "natural" or "more neutral" form of a word is still prevalent among lexicographers, in practice if not in theory. For verb forms, the infinitive is considered to be the default entry, even though, as William J. Frawley, Kenneth C. Hill, and Pamela Munro (2002) point out, these forms are nearly impossible to elicit in a natu-

---

3. Most lexicographers do not make a distinction between the terms *headword* and *lemma*. However, some argue that there is a distinction between the two terms (for more, see Svensén 2009). This book follows general lexicographic convention, using the two terms interchangeably.

4. *Merriam-Webster*, s.v. "teach," s.v. "teacher," s.v. "walk," accessed January 9, 2019, https://www.merriam-webster.com/.

5. Homonyms are words that are spelled the same and pronounced the same but have different meanings. Common examples in English include *second* (after first) and *second* (a measure of time), or *duck* (a bird) and *duck* (an action).

ral setting, even among literate speaker populations who are highly familiar with dictionary formats; if I ask "What are you doing?" in English, the most natural response would be "walking" or "eating" or some other present progressive form. Yet the headwords for these verbs in all major English dictionaries are *walk* and *eat*. The long history of English-language dictionaries has accustomed the user to this stiltedness. But such presumed grammatical structures have led to arbitrary and confusing headwords across the genre, including in many Indigenous-language dictionaries (Pulte and Feeling 2002).

The Tunica Language Project (TLP) had two lexicographic predecessors to consider; these historical Tunica documents, Mary R. Haas's dictionary (1953) and John R. Swanton's vocabulary cards (Gatschet and Swanton n.d.), varied drastically in their determinations of Tunica headword.[6] Swanton's Tunica headwords are determined purely by spelling. All senses, no matter how semantically dissimilar, are listed on the same dictionary card slip. In contrast, Haas's 1953 *Tunica Dictionary* determines headwords based on a mix of etymology and semantics. Related lemmata are nested under a head morpheme. For example, here are the entries that Haas (1953) lists under the head morpheme *háyi* 'old, aged':

> háyi adj. old, aged
>> -háyi st. to be old, aged
>> -háyi m. poss. n. husband. Prob. An attempt to trans. the clq. Term "old man"; the older term for "husband" is -šáyi.
>
> háyi- postp. and adv. stem (TG 5.61 and 5.62) referring to "the top part" in
>> háyihta postp. on, upon, onto, over (-hta on, TG 4.85)
>> háyiši postp. above; adv. above, up, up above (-ši at, TG 4.85)
>>> háyiškɛra adv. backwards, on one's back, in supine position
>>> háyištáʔuruni m. the one who whoops above (mythical being mentioned in TT 8A:f and 8B:e)
>> háyuhuni (read háyihuni ?) adv. G-S above. Cf. háluhuni at the base and híhuni and míhuni yonder.
>
> háyihku adj. different, strange, foreign, alien; various, varied

---

6. Though Swanton did not publish a Tunica dictionary, he prepared for its publication, creating more than three thousand word slips complete with headwords and example sentences (Swanton n.d.; Gatschet and Swanton n.d.).

Haas determines separation of the above words based on semantic relation. Haas (1953) goes so far as to list morphemes as unique headwords even if their meaning is not known. In the example below, *kiri* appears as two lemmata. The first is of unknown meaning and only appears once, in a compound form; the second is of meaning "to grind."

> -kíri occurring only in nárakíri king snake
> kíri tr. to grind . . . (e.g., coffee, corn)
>> kíri adj. ground
>> tákiri (agent.) "grinder" in káfitákiri coffee mill
>> kíri. . c. tr. G-S to grind. . . . equivalent to kíri, used by Y, but kíri. . c. is
>>> prob. the older form.
>>> tákirini (agent.) "grinder" in háhkatákirini gristmill and káfitákirini
>>>> coffee mill

As seen in this example, the headword for the second form of *kiri* is the transitive verb sense. If a lemma contains senses with different parts of speech, Haas (1953) always lists the verb sense as the headword. This decision stems from her determination that the verb is the underived form, and that all other forms (nouns, adjectives, etc.) are derivative. As seen above, Haas deviates from pure alphabetization, listing *takiri* and *takirini* under *kiri*. These words are not listed under the letter T; this is the only place they appear on the Tunica–English side of the dictionary. For a user to arrive at this place in Haas's dictionary, she must have some basic understanding of Tunica morphology.

The New Tunica Dictionary deviates from Swanton's and Haas's headword determinations in significant ways. The first decision made was to include all compound words, such as *takiri* and *takirini*, as their own headwords in the alphabetically expected location. While this decision causes its own problems—namely, all agentive constructions[7] start with *ta-* and are thus clustered together in the dictionary—it requires little analysis from the dictionary user. If the user encounters these forms in Tunica texts, he can quickly find the meaning in the dictionary.

---

7. *Agentive* is a linguistic term that denotes the doer of an action. In English, the agentive is expressed by the suffix *-er*. The person who sings is a *singer*. The machine that prints is a *printer*. In Tunica, the agentive is expressed with the prefix *ta-*, and *hara* 'to sing' becomes *tahara* 'singer'.

Given the range of Tunica familiarity among the users of the new dictionary, we felt it important to accommodate even the newest of Tunica speakers, as repeated unsuccessful lookups could drive potential users away from the using the dictionary or, possibly, learning the language.

Along a similar line of reasoning, we decided that the Tunica–English side of the dictionary would include all irregular word forms as their own headword, even if grammatically related. For example, derived forms of the irregular stative verb *erusa* appear as their own headwords so that users can quickly find the entry and corresponding meaning if they come across these words in Tunica texts. In the example that follows, note that the entries do not appear together in this grouping in the dictionary but are rather widely dispersed, alphabetized by first letter.

> **erusa** *v.st* know, I know: this verb is irregular, see appendix for grammatical info. *"Tahɔhkaheluni ihkeni kitap'ɛnhch, erusa kashi yanik'ahcha,"* *nikatɛni.* "If I put my hand in the hole, I will know for sure," she said.
>
> **erunasa** *cf.* **erusa** *v.st* we know
>
> **herunasa** *cf.* **erusa** *v.st* you all know (f)
>
> **herusa** *cf.* **erusa** *v.st* you know (f)
>
> **orunasa** *cf.* **erusa** *v.st* they know (2m)
>
> **orusa** *cf.* **erusa** *v.st* he knows
>
> **serunasa** *cf.* **erusa** *v.st* they know (f)
>
> **serusa** *cf.* **erusa** *v.st* they all know (m)
>
> **terusa** *cf.* **erusa** *v.st* she knows
>
> **werusa** *cf.* **erusa** *v.st* you know (m)
>
> **werunasa** *cf.* **erusa** *v.st* you all know (m)

The main entry, *erusa*, still carries the most information, and motivated dictionary users are rewarded with additional grammar information and example sentences should they make use of the cross-referencing. Still, the derived headwords have enough information to stand on their own. In contrast, we did not include derived forms of *erusa* as glosses on the English–Tunica side of the dictionary, although we did include an in-line note to direct users to the dictionary's appendix for assistance on verb forms. Since English–Tunica is the production side of the dictionary, we felt confident that any user seeking to create Tunica would have other resources available to aid in derivation.

know **erusa*, **erunasa* *v.st* [this verb is highly irregular, see appendix]

"*Tahɔhkaheluni ihkeni kitap'ɛnhch, erusa kashi yanik'ahcha," nikatɛni.* "If
I put my hand in the hole, I will know for sure," she said.

As can be seen from these entries, the New Tunica Dictionary is not tied to symmetrical or uniform entries. Instead we prioritized function to guide our headword determinations where appropriate.

One final important question to consider when determining headwords is whether to use a strategy called elicitation. This method of headword selection involves giving a speaker a list of words (often nouns) and having her give their Indigenous-language counterparts. We did not use this method for the New Tunica Dictionary, but it was utilized by earlier Tunica scholars, and I have talked to several groups that have adopted this strategy as a means of filling out their dictionaries. Lexicographic programs such as FLEx have prebuilt word lists arranged by semantic domain that can be printed out and entered systematically. This approach can certainly result in lots of lexicographic data in a short period of time. However, elicitation as a methodology has its limitations. Field linguists have found results to be unreliable and sometimes contradictory when terms are elicited out of context (Chelliah 2001; Crowley 2007). There is also a danger of melding or altogether missing linguistic concepts as the elicitor's knowledge (or lack of knowledge) of the target language can skew results (Sapir 1921). A subset of the older Tunica materials was clearly compiled using this method, resulting in broad gaps in domains such as kinship and time. For example, Albert S. Gatschet (1886a) archived his elicitation lists; in them we see a list that asks about words for *mother* and *father* as spoken by a daughter or son. But it does not ask speakers of both genders about siblings. Consequently, Gatschet only recorded sibling vocabulary from a male perspective (the gender of his consultant), missing words and concepts spoken by female speakers. Haas mixed elicitation using photographs as prompts with analyses of longer texts and stories. She ultimately withheld some words collected via elicitation, such as *onitasaku* 'man eater' for "shark," which appears in Haas's field notebooks but was not included in her dictionary slips or published dictionary. We have no insight into why she decided to exclude these headwords, other than her overarching belief that Tunica vocabulary could be doubtful in its authenticity, and perhaps a belief that her interlocutor, Sesostrie Youchigant, would rather create a Tunica neologism on the spot than provide no gloss.

If possible (and I fully recognize that it is not always possible or appropriate), lexicographers who use the lexical elicitation method should augment this process with text elicitation or corpus lexicography; use of a corpus or analyzed texts in determining headwords can help the lexicographer cross-reference elicited forms and perhaps fill in word forms that did not appear when a noncommunity lexicographer was in the driver's seat of elicitation. The danger of lexicon elicitations is their lack of context, but thoughtfully considered elicitation strategies can be helpful in filling in dictionary headwords, particularly when the lexicographer is familiar enough with the language to recognize stilted or missing language data.

Part of Speech and Other Grammatical Information

Part of speech inclusion is a topic of debate among lexicographers of bilingual dictionaries. Assuming the dictionary is between a user's native (L1) and non-native language (L2), a lexicographer must determine how much grammatical information will be included in each side of the dictionary. The heart of the debate centers on the question of whether the dictionary will include ample grammatical information about the languages so that it can stand alone as an independent resource, or whether the user will be expected to consult other texts.

Part of speech is most helpful when going from a user's L1 to L2. I can assume that a native speaker of English is not helped by the information that *breathe* is a regular intransitive verb; they know how to categorize and conjugate it without an extraneous identifier. But I cannot assume that the user will know that its counterpart, *hɛha*, is of the rare intransitive Tishlina verb class.[8] Or that *wana* and *ɛlu* are stative verbs, especially given that their English counterparts, *want* and *like*, have a

---

8. Tishlina class verbs describe circumstances or states that happen to someone. There are two types of Tishlina verbs, transitive and intransitive. Both types have a feminine subject as the actor. Intransitive Tishlina verbs denote nonvolitional states or actions, such as the passage of time. The English-language phrase "it is 2 o'clock" would, in Tunica, be *Wirant'ɛ ilihta pirati* (lit. "she turned the second hour"). Transitive Tishlina verbs denote involuntary actions, such as coughing, sweating, or losing while gambling. For example, *Ihkhiyuti* 'I woke up' literally translates to "She woke me" (more examples in Anderson and Maxwell, forthcoming).

more active alignment. To that end, all Tunica headwords—and all Tunica translations in the English–Tunica side—of our dictionary include parts of speech, while English words include no such documentation. This choice to always include part of speech for Tunica words helps users produce the correct Tunica form, especially if the parts of speech are not congruous across languages. For example, here is the English–Tunica entry for *earthquake*:

> **earthquake** halihila *v.I.intr Halihil'una*. There was an earthquake. Literally, they two (Red and Blue Alligator) earthquaked. [Red Alligator and Blue Alligator are responsible for Tunica seasons; when both move, the earth quakes.]

Earthquake is not marked as an English noun, but its Tunica counterpart is called out as a verb. The hope is that this information is enough for a user to effectively produce the Tunica word form that describes earthquakes.

The abbreviations used to indicate part of speech were the subject of a deliberate conversation that I brought to the Tunica working group. We discussed the following questions:

> What is our overall approach to part of speech conventions? Do we want to indicate low-level grammatical gradation such as "transitive Class II verb"? Or is "Class II verb" or even just "verb" sufficiently informative to most dictionary users?
>
> Would the abbreviations be based on Tunica or English glosses?
>
> Would abbreviations be identical on both sides of the dictionary?

KYLY came up with a comprehensive list of abbreviations based on both English and Tunica vocabulary. While ultimately the Tunica abbreviations were not used in the dictionary itself, which instead relied solely on English-based abbreviations, the conversation resulted in many neologisms that have since been used in other pedagogical resources. The expansion of Tunica into the domain of technical linguistics resulted in the vocabulary and abbreviations seen in table 1.

In addition to part of speech, another challenge encountered in practical lexicographic design is grammatical information: how much grammatical information should be included in dictionary entries? Phonological rules, verbal paradigms,

Table 1. Part of Speech Determinations

English Term	Tunica Term	Abbr. Eng.	Abbr. Tun.
noun	*taka*	n	tk
pronoun	*takat (taka + -hat)*	pro	tkt
adjective	*taka halani*	adj	tkh
adverb	*taya halani*	adv	tyh
postposition	*ahkihtaku*	post	ahki
interrogative-indefinite (*kata, kaku*, etc.)	*yoluyanaka*	int	yyk
singular	*sahku*	s	s
dual	*ili*	d	i
plural	*namu*	p	n
collective	*kuhpani*	c	kp
1st person	*onisahku*	1	1
2nd person	*onili*	2	2
3rd person	*onenihku*	3	3
masculine	*ku*	m	ku
feminine	*hchi*	f	hchi
mixed group (masc./fem.)	*hotu*	mf	hotu
verb	*taya*	v	ty
intransitive verb	*tayalɔta*	v.intr	tyl
transitive verb	*tayanahchu*	v.tr	tyn
completive	*yati*	comp	ti
habitual	*yakati*	hab	kati
imperative	*waka*	imp	w
durative	*yuru*	dur	yur
Class I verb	*korini sahku*	v.I	ty.ks
Class II verb	*korini ili*	v.II	ty.ki
Stative verb	*tayawana*	v.st	ty.w
Stative inchoative verb	*tayapira*	v.st.i	ty.p
Tahch'i Rahihta verb	*Tahch'i Rahihta*	v.TR	ty.TR
Tishlina verb	*Tishlina*	v.T	ty.T

Note: The abbreviations above can be combined to give a user more detailed information about a headword's part of speech. The most common combinations are as follows: v.I.intr=Class I intransitive verb, v.II.tr=Class II transitive verb, v.TR.f=feminine Tahch'i Rahihta verb, v.TR.m=masculine Tahch'i Rahihta verb, v.TR.m.II=masculine Class II Tahch'i Rahihta verb, v.T.intr=intransitive Tishlina verb, v.T.tr=transitive Tishlina verb.

and other morphological complexities may clutter the field of vision and affect a user's ability to find a lemma or use it properly. The expected user's knowledge of the language and ability to consult outside sources also factor into a lexicographer's decision about these grammatical aspects. Some lexicographers expect that dictionary users are familiar with regular features of inflection, and that dictionaries only need to include irregular inflection. However, this view has fallen out of favor in contemporary lexicography, especially among those engaged with bilingual and pedagogical lexicography (Svensén 2009, 125). Modern dictionaries tend toward including all the information a user would need to become fully informed about a word without consulting other texts. This tendency is particularly pronounced in revitalization lexicography, as resources in the form of printed texts or proficient speakers may be difficult to come by. Nevertheless, lexicographers disagree on where in the dictionary grammatical information should appear. Placing the information within the entry itself has the advantage of immediate juxtaposition with the headword, reducing the likelihood of misuse. However, these additional notations can clutter a dictionary entry if a great amount of grammatical information is needed. Alternatively, verbal paradigms can be included in an appendix, front matter, or other places outside of the entry (Svensén 2009). In the New Tunica Dictionary, irregular grammatical information accompanies lemmata; a more complete account of Tunica's phonological and morphological processes is found in a pedagogical grammar sketch in the dictionary's front matter, as well as in a quick reference guide in the dictionary's appendix.

Spelling and Pronunciation

Some lexicographers see spelling and pronunciation as core functions of the dictionary. Given the authority dictionaries possess to dictate "good" and "bad" language, the exclusion of spelling variations can influence how users value orthographic variation in the language. Orthographic differences in legacy Tunica materials posed a challenge for KYLY, prompting us to grapple with how we wanted the language to be presented to Tunica learners. For example, Gatschet (1886a) recorded "bad" as *lähähä*; Swanton (1921) preferred the spelling *lapoho*; and Haas (1940) wrote the word *lap'ɔhɔ*. By the time our Tunica dictionary project had begun, three years after the start of the overall language revitalization project, the group had settled on an orthography and agreed that Haas's orthographic determinations would be deemed the authoritative standard.[9] Therefore, most spelling disputes were settled on the basis of authorship.

However, Haas did not shy away from documenting variation in her 1953 dictionary. Cognizant that she was working with the last speaker, she diligently recorded variations in pronunciation that she considered to be significant. Some such variations were exclusive to the materials of Gatschet and Swanton, whose accuracy in phonetics was questionable, but an equal number were given by Youchigant. When a variant showed up between the data sets, Haas made note of it, using the label "G-S" to indicate Gatschet and Swanton:

> tɛhpa, tɛhpa. . c. tr. to touch . . . Var. táhpa, táhpa. . c., but note that tɛhpa is
> found in G-S

One discussion among KYLY members concerned the extent to which allophonic variations should be encouraged. From the outset, it was determined that all variations would be present in the Tunica–English side, but that some might be marked as "obsolete" with a cross-reference to the contemporary form. A variant was favored by KYLY if it was corroborated in Gatschet and Swanton's cards, an aspect that Haas generally noted, as seen in *tɛhpa*, above.

Notably, the group did not prefer forms that were present in Gatschet and Swanton's cards but uncorroborated in Haas's data unless the G-S variant could be explained by a widespread phonological feature. For example, *tepusa* 'polite' is a G-S form not accepted by Youchigant, who uses *tipusa*. In this instance, the latter is preferred because the group felt that Haas had a better ear and more consistently documented the difference between /e/ and /i/, whereas G-S forms were riddled with inconsistency surrounding vowels even for the same words recorded in a single document. However, in cases of phonetic variation that would be explained by rapid language loss, the group preferred the earlier form. One example arose when dealing with pre-aspiration, or consonant clusters that began with /h/, such as *hk, ht,* and *hp*. Pre-aspiration is meaningful in Tunica, resulting in words with different meaning, for example *mahka* 'dear' or 'to fall in love' and *maka* 'fat'. When entering

---

9. Haas's subsequent, robust documentation of other Indigenous languages proved that she was a far more astute and consistent scholar than her earlier counterparts, with a "stunningly sharp ear" for phonetics (McLendon 1997, 522).

headwords into the dictionary, I noticed a number of words recorded by Haas as lacking pre-aspiration, with a note that the G-S variant contained pre-aspiration. Take, for example, Haas's entry *tépi* and its subentry *ʔatépi*, seen below.

-tépi in
>   ʔatépi adv. joined together; together; side by side (in G-S written
>   ʔatéhpi) (ʔa-, TG 4.562)
>   tépi. . c., usually with ʔa-, reciprocal pref. intr. to join together, connect

Haas lists only *tépi* (and not *téhpi*) in the dictionary, but her mention of pre-aspiration in the G-S form under *ʔatépi* led KYLY to believe that pre-aspiration was likely present in the standalone form, even if Youchigant never pronounced it. KYLY made *tehpi* the preferred form in the New Tunica Dictionary based on a consensus that pre-aspiration was indeed a widespread feature of Tunica, and its disappearance in this environment can be explained by rapid language loss in a context where the "killer" languages do not have phonemic or meaningful pre-aspiration. KYLY thus attempted to leverage the authority of the dictionary to stem the tide of language change or reaffirm the legitimacy of older word forms, a strategy also used in other Indigenous-language revitalization efforts (Rice and Saxon 2002; Warner, Butler, and Luna-Costillas 2006).

When Youchigant vacillated between forms documented in G-S and non-G-S materials, we used the G-S-corroborated form for the associated entry in the New Tunica Dictionary. Take, for example, the Haas (1953) entries for *kuhu* and *uhu*, both meaning "to cough":

kúhu intr. or trsimp. to cough. Also given as ʔúhu; Y alternated between
>   kúhu and ʔúhu in this mng., but ʔúhu occurs in G-S.
ʔúhu intr. or trsimp. to cough. Also given once or twice as kúhu, but ʔúhu
>   is the stem occurring in G-S in this mng.

In this case, *kuhu* is clearly an anomaly. It could have been a momentary memory lapse on the part of the consultant or an analytic error on the part of the linguist.[10]

---

10. There is good evidence that Haas incorrectly analyzed object markers on certain verbs, resulting in initial /k/ or /hk/ consonant clusters. For further reading, see Heaton (2016).

Regardless, the older form, *uhu*, is the preferred form in the New Tunica Dictionary, appearing as the only entry under *cough* in the production-focused English–Tunica side.

In general, we omitted forms that Haas (1953) marked as "doubtful," "rare," or "incorrect" if there was a viable alternative. For example, here are Haas's entries for *hohči* 'to limp' and *horu* 'to exchange, swap', as well as their variants. Haas indicates uncertainty through the use of notations in the entries themselves and an associated note:

> hóhči trsimp. (rarely intr.) to limp. Var. hóhču
>
> hóhču rare var. (perh. incorrect) of hóhči to limp
>
> hólu. . c. Dft., probably intended for hóru to exchange . . .
>
> hóru tr. G-S to exchange, swap . . .
>> Note: Y once gave a stem hólu. . c. in this mng. but later failed to recognize it; perh. he was trying to recall hóru.

In such instances, we made the less-doubtful form the preferred word (here, we exclusively listed *hohchi* and *horu* in the dictionary). However, there were some instances when we retained a word that Haas (1953) had labeled as "doubtful," "rare," or "incorrect." If the doubted word had no alternative or variant form, we kept it in the dictionary and removed its label, with the goal of encouraging its use in contemporary Tunica. This is yet another way the dictionary wields its authority in legitimizing language, bringing language that was once considered outlier into mainstream use.

Definition or Gloss

Once the headword is determined, a lexicographer must decide how to define or gloss a term. Given the nature of the New Tunica Dictionary, our project focused on bilingual glosses from one language to the other with minimal explanation of the meaning when possible. In bilingual dictionaries, the definition can be complicated by linguistic equivalence or overlapping meaning in the two languages. Equivalence between two languages can range from full equivalence, where there is complete agreement between expressions in meaning and usage (a rare occurrence), to zero equivalence, where the target language does not have the concept of a given word in the source language. Most often words and expressions fall within the range of partial equivalence, having some semantic overlap coupled with semantic or pragmatic divergence (Svensén 2009). For example, the Tunica word *rihku* corresponds to the English words *wood, wooden, woods, forest, tree, stick,* and *log.* The apocopated Tunica variant *tarku* maps only to *forest* or *woods* and is often used phrasally, as in the collocation *tarku kichu* 'into the woods'. The amount of information that we included about *rihku* and *tarku* hinged on whether Tunica was the target or source language, and on whether the dictionary half in which it appeared primarily facilitated production, reception, or both. Our chosen entries for *rihku* and the corresponding English term *forest* were as follows (the English–Tunica side also included separate entries for the other meanings of *rihku,* not reproduced here):

Tunica–English
rihku 1) *n* log **2)** *n* stick **3)** *n* tree **4)** *n* forest; woods **5)** *n* wood **6)** *adj* wood, wooden
tarku kichu *post* in the woods

English–Tunica
forest tarku *n* [often in "tarku kichu" *post*]; rihku *n*

Equivalence goes beyond simple denotative meaning; a bilingual dictionary must offer insight into the pragmatic use of words. Haas (1953) envisioned that her dictionary would be used for translating Tunica texts. While she included ample extralinguistic information on the Tunica–English side, she put none on the English–Tunica side. This lack of contextualization on the English–Tunica side can lead to issues. Take, for example, the following two entries, both related to the word *sari* 'to be full of hate':

Tunica–English
sári tr. to hate, detest, abhor . . . ; st. to be extremely angry, full of hate
  Note: To use this term is equivalent to cursing. It is never used when
     speaking to a child.

English–Tunica
hate, to be full of -sári

In Tunica, *sari* has strong connotations on par with swearing and would never be used in conversations with a child; these connotations are, conversely, not common to the notion of hatred in English. Without this connotative information explicitly marked in the English–Tunica side of the dictionary, English speakers who are producing Tunica will change the meaning of *sari* or offend those who are familiar with the connotative meaning. In contrast with Haas's dictionary, the New Tunica Dictionary includes such pragmatic information on both language sides.

KYLY felt strongly that because our dictionary was intended be pedagogical, connotations of religious or cultural practices that are not widely accessible or understood by users should be explicitly outlined within entries. For example, the Tunica word *mɛka* is glossed by Haas (1953) as "to have bad luck, receive punishment due to failure to fast or observe religious rites." This entry is accompanied by a long explanation of the important religious significance of this word, though "Youchigant found it impossible to render [*mɛka*] adequately into either French or English." While incomplete, this definition provides important religious context that is unfamiliar to contemporary Tunica speakers. In the New Tunica Dictionary, we recorded the religious aspect of *mɛka* by providing information on historical fasting rituals, stating that *mɛka* could happen if a person did not observe such rites. On the Tunica–English side, this information appears as a subentry for *mɛka* (along with other glosses provided by Haas, such as *unlucky*). On the English–Tunica side, the extended entry for *mɛka* appears under the English noun *fast*, thus preserving the information even though we do not have a fully equivalent meaning in English.

Indeed, dictionaries offer a unique opportunity to document cultural practices that survive in the language though they are dwindling in society at large. This observation is supported by other Indigenous-language lexicographers, such as Gabriele H. Cablitz (2011), who argues that cultural information *must* be included in Indigenous-language dictionaries because the speaker population cannot be assumed to still have access to the cultural knowledge behind the terms. This need can be particularly urgent in language communities where cultural practices are diminishing from generation to generation. In the case of Tunica, several words that were recorded by earlier scholars no longer have enough context for their meanings to be deciphered. For example, *shahkani* was documented by Gatschet to mean "an old Indian game" in which "marked pieces of wood were shuffled up in cotton and bets were made on which side would appear uppermost" (Haas 1953, s.v. "šahkani"). However, Gatschet left out many details such as the lengths of wood that were used, the rules for betting, the size of bets, and the general purpose of and social setting for this game. Was it played recreationally, or, like stickball, used to settle disputes? By the time Youchigant was working with Haas in the 1930s, he could not recall the specifics of the game, and contemporary Tunica people have not retained any knowledge of its rules. The opportunity to fully document the pragmatic and cultural context of this game was lost. Yet the word remains in the Tunica lexicon, as there is a possibility that someone someday will uncover more information about the game.

I am the first to admit that the inclusion of cultural or religious information and vocabulary is not appropriate for all communities. Some communities encompass words or practices that are not to be shared with noncommunity members or whose knowledge is held by practitioners or subgroup members (Hill 2002). Other communities adhere to strict taboos of what time of year or season certain knowledge can be spoken aloud (Toelken 1998). Others may have taboos around sharing the images or voices of elders who have recently died, thus requiring any digital material accompanying a multimedia dictionary entry to be restricted (Ogilvie 2011b). There are many well-documented accounts of communities deciding to exclude or obfuscate aspects of dictionary material due to concerns about who would have access to that information (e.g., Debenport 2015; Yurok Language Project 2017). Digital dictionaries can offer some reprieve for communities that require information be withheld from unauthorized users by necessitating passwords or disabling access at certain times of the year. Yet even so, to enable these features, the lexicographer must store the knowledge in a database on a computer in some shape or form, which opens it up to possible unauthorized access. Ultimately, the decision to include or exclude cultural and religious information should be in the hands of the linguistic community. It is entirely unethical to input lexicographic entries of which the community has not fully approved. As stated in chapter 1, community processes determining these decisions will likely not be instant, and community members may even disagree among themselves as to the proper course of action. The job of a noncommunity lexicographer is to stand aside and let the community drive the conversation, facilitating discussion or offering opinions only when asked. The community members own their language and their traditional knowledge; and the community has a right to decide how it is represented in all printed materials, dictionary or otherwise.

That said, the TLP and contemporary Tunica learners are grateful for the level of detail included in previous linguistic materials. From ethnobotanical wisdom to traditional dances, many Tunica practices are now being revitalized due to the legacy of ancestral language speakers. The New Tunica Dictionary continues the tradition of describing cultural and religious practices with entries where appropriate.

Example Sentences

Example sentences are considered by some lexicographers to be the crown jewel of a dictionary's microstructure. While there is conflicting evidence as to how often dictionary users actually consult example sentences when looking up words (Laufer 1993; Atkins 1996), lexicographers delight in the potential they contain. And with good reason. Example sentences can elegantly fulfill several functions, both linguistic and ideological: they show how to use a word in context; they can exemplify collocations; they can document or showcase cultural practices relevant to the word; they can reinforce stories or immortalize significant historical events; they can mediate differences in worldview and cosmovision; and they can tell a user how to be a good speaker, both linguistically and practically (Drysdale 1987; Ostermann 2015; Debenport 2015).

Example sentences come in three flavors: (1) *authentic* example sentences, which have been extracted directly from available texts; (2) *constructed* example sentences, which are created by the lexicographer or lexicographic committee to best exemplify common uses or collocations of the word; and (3) a *mixed* approach, where authentic sentences are edited for clarity to highlight the target word.

Historically, consensus among lexicographers was that the "best" example sentence was one plucked from its original context and placed in the dictionary with no alteration to the sentence. From the earliest of European dictionaries, it has been argued that example sentences should be from the most authentic and authoritative sources. However, what constitutes authenticity varies based on time and place. At the height of the eighteenth century, authentic examples meant the "purest" examples of the English language; hence Samuel Johnson's 1755 dictionary drew example sentences from the Bible, as well as from Shakespeare and a few other elevated writers. The *Oxford English Dictionary* has a broader definition of authentic examples and boasts that its sources include magazines, travel journals, diaries, and even the works of an alchemist alongside more established sources. However, even in the *Oxford English Dictionary*, certain sources are given more weight, with the *London Times* and William Shakespeare being by far the largest sources of example sentences, totaling seventy-five thousand citations as of February 2019 (Oxford English Dictionary n.d.b.). Moreover, sole reliance on print sources disregards informal and regional language use and does not consider any language found on the radio, television, or social media. A small handful of print dictionaries include unpublished language usage in their selection of example sentences; one English-language dictionary that embraces nonprinted language use is the *American Heritage Dictionary*, which draws on a panel of native speakers to vote on degrees of acceptability of certain word usages.

Acceptance of adapted or invented examples sentences has steadily gained momentum since the early 1990s (Svensén 2009, 284). Nonauthentic example sentences may be modified versions of language use that is attested in a corpus, or they may be created entirely from scratch by a native speaker of the language. As commercial learner dictionaries continue to gain market shares, lexicographers have debated the extent to which learners benefit from invented example sentences that remove unclear or distracting information. Some lexicographers, such as those at COBUILD (discussed in the previous chapter), argue that editorialized examples strip away valuable information that learners need. Others feel that invented or adapted example sentences have their use, but that editors' conflicting intuition is problematic in deciding the final forms of these sentences (Svensén 2009). Still others believe that a lexicographer's intuition about her native language should not be written off, and that a lexicographer's intuition about example sentence grammaticality and typical word use results in example sentences that have greater pedagogic value than those created from attested language usage in a corpus (Laufer 1992).

The question of authentic and constructed example sentences did not play a contentious role in the creation of the New Tunica Dictionary. Unfortunately, we did not have the luxury of a large print Tunica corpus from which to draw example sentences. Nor could we consult native-speaker intuition. The text corpus of the Tunica language available to me as lexicographer included: (1) a handwritten notebook compiled by Gatschet on Tunica grammar; (2) ten Swanton texts, many of which were copies of Gatschet texts; (3) seventy-five Haas texts of varied length, some spanning pages, others comprising just two sentences; and

(4) fifteen field notebooks of Haas containing elicited Tunica sentences not found in her published *Tunica Texts*.

From the outset of the New Tunica Dictionary, it was understood that a significant set of example sentences would be constructed by hand, as some words do not have sentence attestations in the available texts, and others, in the case of neologisms, have no previous attestation whatsoever. However, KYLY and I agreed that there were benefits to using as many authentic example sentences as possible. Authentic example sentences inherently showcase Tunica cultural practices and exemplify the language as used by native speakers. For example, the following sentence is lifted from the traditional story *Tayoroniku Tahalayihkuku Onti*, "Why the Tunica and Biloxi Became Friends." It exemplifies a clear use of the word *eti* 'friend' and ties the word to an origin story about the Tunica and Biloxi peoples:

*Hinyatihch, Tahalayihkuku, "tahikuwaku ima **eti**," nikɔni.*
"We are **friends** with the panther," said the Biloxi.

> Haas 1950, 148 (put into contemporary Tunica by KYLY)

Drawing from traditional Tunica stories and accounts of day-to-day life contextualizes the language, a boon to the education of intermediate and advanced Tunica speakers. Moreover, most older Tunica sources are neither published nor readily available to Tunica speakers; the use of these texts as example sentences in the dictionary is an opportunity to distribute legacy materials more widely.

However, it was agreed that not all authentic sentences make the best candidates for inclusion in the dictionary. In certain instances, the word is only used once in the available corpus, and the sentence is convoluted. For example, the only occurrence of the word *aka* 'to absorb' in the corpus is as follows:

*Tayatahkishi lapuya uhkkɔsatahch osintalu kichu uhkpan'utahch uhklisumasutahch osintaluhchi lapuya tayatahkishi **aka**tihch uhktar'antahch tarku pasak'uhchutahch uhkhirukatani.*

When they had thoroughly scraped the deer hide, they dipped it in brain [water], [then] squeezed it and twisted it, [and] when the brains had been thoroughly **absorbed** by the deer hide, they stretched it and [then] rubbed it [with] a stick.

> Haas 1951, 162–63

While linguistically and ethnographically informative, this sentence is not ideal for a print dictionary due to its length. Nor is it ideal for a learner, as the target word is buried deep in the sentence structure. In this case, the use of a mixed example sentence strategy made sense: the phrase containing *aka* was pulled out of the larger sentence, leaving us with *osintaluhchi lapuya tayatahkishi **akati***, "the brains had been thoroughly absorbed by the deer hide." An explanatory note tells the dictionary user that this example refers to tanning, a once-common practice among the Tunica.

Remaining completely true to the texts of Haas and Swanton was also problematic due to the genre from which they were collected. Haas in particular relied heavily on Youchigant's storytelling. The storytelling genre has several tropes and stylistic features that were likely not found in informal conversation. For example, nearly every sentence in the *Tunica Texts* (1950) starts with *hinyatihch* 'then' and ends with *-ani* 'it is said, they say'. The high frequency of these words in authentic example sentences is likely disproportionate to the actual frequency of use. Just as no English speaker starts a conversation about their childhood by saying "Once upon a time," Tunica speakers would not start every conversational sentence with *hinyatihch*. This realization prompted me to modify authentic example sentences to demonstrate a more balanced representation of storytelling style and everyday conversation.

Ultimately, many example sentences in the New Tunica Dictionary are "inspired" example sentences: sentences that appear in Tunica textual sources but are in some way modified from their original context. Many more were constructed to highlight common use and collocations. These sentences draw from a variety of cultural knowledge, ranging from descriptions of pow-wow regalia to non-Indigenous fairy tales. In the examples below, the headword is bolded for easy identification.

*Nikirhipushi hipukuhch, Desmondku **tahki** ohniyutirishitapachuku yamaku.*
When he dances at the Pow-wow, Desmond wears a **bone** breastplate.

*Aparush sa tika hahkakiri shuwiwi. **Sahatetiku** mashuwi.*
A big dog scattered cornmeal in the sky. He made the **Milky Way** (the Dog's Way).

*Tacharinaku ɔnchayihchi hiputi, aparush wichitiman, **tahch'ihchi** pirati.*
The Kingfisher's wife danced, ascended into the sky, and became the **sun.**

Tihpulashi tashihpihchi *Ingrasa nisara rikini tastihpulashi atahchi Sally*
   Ridehchi tetisa.
The youngest U.S. **astronaut** to go the stars was Sally Ride.

Yaruhk'osini *ihkarahch, sehi pɛkan'i. Tɔha pɛkan'i. Hɛhali tepɛkan'i.*
If I had a **hammer**, I'd hammer in the morning. I'd hammer in the evening.
   I'd hammer all over this land.

Cinderellahchi tɛshkalahpi lahpiti **romantohku.**
Cinderella **easily** put her shoe on.

All example sentences were constructed by a dedicated example-sentence working group and were presented to the larger revitalization team before inclusion
in the digital dictionary; all will be approved by representatives of the Tunica-
Biloxi Tribal Council before final publication in print format.[11] Given the bounty
of information that is conveyed via example sentences, community stakeholders
should be fully involved with their selection. The online dictionary was initially
published in 2017 without example sentences; as of 2020 and the writing of this
book, editing and vetting of Tunica example sentences are ongoing, and approved
examples sentences are published to the app version of the dictionary biannually.
The print dictionary will be released once all edited example sentences have been
approved by Tunica-Biloxi tribal elders.

Microstructure and Language Standardization

Discussed in the last chapter, a key function that the TLP identified for the new
dictionary was language standardization. The microstructure of an entry was a
crucial point in which this function was realized. Standardization of the language
was taking place outside of the dictionary project; these community discussions
had to be realized in the dictionary because the forms that appear in a dictionary

---

11. The opportunity to construct example sentences was made available to all members of
KYLY and many Tunica learners through the annual immersion workshops. However, most
example sentences were ultimately constructed and grammatically verified by a core group
that consisted of Judith Maxwell, Donna Pierite, and me, in my capacity as head lexicographer.

become the yardstick against which other language use is measured. Additionally, the dictionary's compilation drove many discussions regarding standard spellings and verb classes.

KYLY felt that the presence of standard forms as they appear in the dictionary would benefit the revitalization effort in a number of ways: (1) it ensures that new learners are using common vocabulary, grammatical rules, and orthographies for mutual intelligibility; (2) standardization opens the door for the dictionary's use in public education settings, which require a standard language and curriculum; and (3) standardized grammatical patterns make the language easier to learn and understand. These goals differ from Haas's (1953) objective: describe the language in the fullest manner possible before the last speaker passes away. Haas was not deterred from recording ambiguous, incomplete, or even conflicting information in her 1953 dictionary since ambiguities and incongruities were given to her by her consultant. From her copious field notes, it is apparent that Haas pursued these inconstancies as far as she could, asking Youchigant follow-up questions in the moment and reviewing every single dictionary card with him before publication. However, there were still instances in which Youchigant could not remember a form he had given previously, or in which he gave inconsistent answers to the same question. In some cases, Youchigant insisted that his seemingly incompatible ways of using grammar were correct, a strong indicator that the Tunica language was undergoing language change even as it was losing speakers and falling silent. For example, Tunica has robust grammatical gender, and all nouns are inherently assigned one lexical gender, masculine or feminine. However, in the case of *asa* 'tail', Youchigant inflected it as feminine in most stories, but occasionally inflected it as masculine. Haas's field notes indicate that she tried to clarify this glaring contradiction with Youchigant, but he had no explanation. Consequently, Haas dutifully recorded all that Youchigant said, regardless of any conflict, noting when Youchigant later forgot a word, used a doubtful variant, or did not recognize words recorded by earlier language consultants.

The rampant inconsistencies documented in certain aspects of the Tunica language, such as the grammatical gender of inanimate nouns, is unsurprising and, in fact, expected. Carmel O'Shannessy (2011) describes the common process of language change and attrition during periods of language shift. It is remarkable that Youchigant, having no other speakers with whom to converse, remembered as much as he did. Haas's extensive analysis on the language gives us a clear picture of most of its features. However, the devil is in the details, and ambiguities in sweeping aspects of the language make it difficult for contemporary language learners to absorb the language and use it consistently. It was clear from the outset of the TLP that certain grammatical features would need to be examined and standardized for contemporary language use.

To that end, KYLY has made several decisions over the course of revitalization that affect Tunica structure. In some instances, the changes made in the name of standardization have radically altered underlying grammatical forms, making contemporary Tunica entirely different from what one finds in Youchigant's Tunica. Other modifications are minor and serve to unmask and highlight distinctive features long present in Tunica. For example, Tunica has a grammatical distinction between alienable possession (in which nouns can exist independently, without a possessor) and inalienable possession (in which nouns must always mark their possessor). Certain Tunica nouns can never be expressed without being possessed, particularly nouns referring to body parts and family members. The prefixes that denote these two types of possession differ only by an /hk/ consonant cluster; *ihk-* 'my', *tihk-* 'hers', and *sihk-* 'theirs' are alienable prefixes, while *i-*, *ti-*, and *si-* are the inalienable prefixes with the same English gloss. However, Haas documented that the distinguishing /hk/ consonant cluster of alienable possession would often be elided due to phonological rules (Haas 1940, 25), which means that a learner who expected to see the alienable word *ihkri* 'my house' would instead see the inalienable-looking *iri*. As part of revitalization, KYLY opted to keep an orthographic distinction between alienable and inalienable pronominal prefixes; in documented Tunica, KYLY felt that highlighting this important Tunica feature justified a change to its phonological rules, leading to the consistent appearance of the /hk/ consonant cluster. This decision cascaded into further reanalysis and subsequent reinterpretation of Tunica. In one instance, a new analysis of the person marker on stative verbs led KYLY to understand that stative verbs beginning with /h/ had been misinterpreted by Haas (Heaton 2016). Due to this finding, certain headwords that started with /h/ in her dictionary are listed without this initial letter in the New Tunica Dictionary: *h'ipota* and *htohkuni*, for example, are now *ipota* and *tohkuni*, respectively.

As head lexicographer, I was tasked with keeping abreast of all decisions that would affect headword representation. KYLY continues to proliferate new standards throughout the community, teaching them in classrooms, and using them in pedagogical materials. Incorporating community-owned standardization ensures that the dictionary is useful and that the standard forms permeate beyond the dictionary. Conversely, entering headwords into FLEx for lexicographic use prompted many conversations about language standardization. Questions about ambiguous parts of speech, spelling variations, and doubtful meanings were brought to KYLY for deliberation. This section deals with the aspects of language standardization insofar as they affected the lexicographic process. Decisions outlined here were made in full collaboration with KYLY; I raised lexicographic questions with the larger group on a regular basis, with some discussions on word form and meaning spanning several weeks. In rare cases, temporary decisions were made at my sole discretion. These decisions are explicitly noted here and in FLEx as they are tagged for further review by the community in future editing cycles.

Standardization of Verb Class

Verb class is a central feature of the Tunica language, determining inflection, semantics, and use of Tunica verbs. Verbs in Tunica can be either Class I or Class II, and this distinction affects how they are conjugated. For example, the first-person plural subject *we* is indicated with *-iti* for Class I verbs (as in *pit'iti* 'we walked') and *-inta* for Class II verbs (as in *sam'inta* 'we cooked'). Tunica speakers are taught that Class I and Class II verbs are distinct in their meanings and use. Most Tunica verbs are inherently Class I. Some verbs are inherently Class II. Other verbs can be both classes, in which case the meaning of the verb changes. The classic example is *hara*, which as a Class I verb means "to sing," but as a Class II verb means "to play a musical instrument."

However, as Haas (1953, 183) notes in the introduction to her dictionary, Tunica verb classes are not so simple: some verbs are used "now as causatives [Class II], now as non-causatives [Class I], without change of meaning." Determining how to handle these verbs was one of the first tasks I undertook as lexicographer, and KYLY discussed whether we should retain the ambiguity of verb class for these words in the dictionary. Upon further probing, I discovered that Haas also noted which of the two forms was more common by listing this form first. Haas used a label of ".. c." to indicate a Class II verb, and she left verbs unmarked if they were Class I. In the following dictionary entry, Haas has indicated that the Class II verb is more common:

sáhi. . c. sáhi tr. to throw . . . (over the shoulder); to pitch . . . (over the
shoulder)

While Haas explicitly states that an entry with the Class II form listed first mean
that this form is seen more frequently in her data (1953, 185), she does not say
anything about the opposite ordering, in which the Class II form comes second.
For example:

wála, wála. . c. to split . . . , split . . . lengthwise

The lack of comment as to what this ordering denotes is a problem for revitalization. KYLY knew from examining Haas's other texts that she considered the Class
I form to be "unmarked" or default. Given the weight that Haas gives Class I forms,
she may be indicating that the Class I form is more common, or that Class I and
Class II uses of the verb are equally as common. Because most of Haas's data is
not currently machine searchable,[12] this inherent ambiguity raised questions for
the group. How would learners decide on which form to use? Is there a form that
KYLY prefers that they use? Or does KYLY want to standardize these verbs in such
a way that they are assigned to a single verb class?

The danger in including both classes as options in the dictionary is that Tunica
learners are primed to prefer Class I inflection. Learners are introduced to Class
I verbs before Class II verbs, and there is a sense among teachers and students
that Class I inflection is "easier." The outcome feared by KYLY was that Class II
forms would fall completely out of use with these verbs if learners were given
a choice. But neither did the group want to dictate a single verb class for these
entries. What if users were consulting the dictionary for forms seen in older texts?
Ultimately, the new dictionary states a "preferred form" that aligns with Haas's
observations about frequency. The more common form is listed as the default
part of speech, immediately following the headword. A bracketed note at the
end of the entry lets users know that other verb classes are allowed, but that the

----

12. The author and coresearchers from the American Philosophical Society in Philadelphia recently won a multi-year grant from the National Science Foundation to digitize Haas's
archival materials and make them searchable using the contemporary Tunica orthography;
the digitization project, which kicks off in August 2020, should provide answers to such questions in the future.

default form is the most common. Here is one such example from the New Tunica Dictionary:

amari₃ *v.II.tr* to measure [This verb can also be Class I, but Class II is preferred]

The Tunica–English entry, shown here, allows for Class I usage in addition to the preferred Class II. Conversely, the corresponding English–Tunica entry lists only Class II. This pattern, in which the production side of the dictionary lists only the preferred form, encourages this form's proliferation in contemporary Tunica.

Another verb class reanalysis due to lexicographic probing concerned what are called Tishlina verbs, which generally describe actions that are involuntary or volitionless. At issue were certain verbs that Haas marked as both Class I intransitive verbs and transitive Tishlina verbs (or what she called "transimpersonals," abbreviated as "trsimp."). Here is Haas's entry for *hɛha* 'to breathe':

hɛha intr. or trsimp. to breathe

In such cases, the order of the class indicators does not vary. These verbs are equally Class I intransitives and transitive Tishlina verbs. In fact, nearly all transitive Tishlina verbs that have to do with involuntary bodily actions such as breathing, belching, coughing, sweating, gasping, twitching (of the eye), getting an erection, sneezing, and vomiting are also listed as intransitive verbs (Haas 1953). In contrast, transitive Tishlina verbs unrelated to bodily functions, such as *lihcha* 'to get wet' and *lahpa* 'to get scalded', do not have a Class I intransitive variation listed. Why the difference in these domains? While we have no definitive answer, it is likely that long contact with European languages and a growing number of native Tunica–French bilinguals had instigated a shift in the language. Tunica had been in contact with Western European languages for nearly two hundred years at the time of Haas's work, and Youchigant himself was a native speaker of French as well as of Tunica. These European-contact languages (French, English, and Spanish) make no distinctions of volition when inflecting verbs; breathing, sneezing, vomiting, and so forth are all active verbs. A shift away from the more passive transimpersonal construction makes grammatical sense. However, other verbs that align with a passive construction, such as getting scalded, remained firmly transimpersonal. While it is possible that this shift was unique to Youchigant, it is plausible that this process had been ongoing. The dearth of Tunica speakers would have accelerated this change. The early historical records of Gatschet and Swanton seem to support this hypothesis. Words such as *sipi* 'to shiver' appear only as transimpersonal verbs (a.k.a. transitive Tishlina verbs); there is no indication that they were used as active Class I verbs at the turn of the century. Haas marks these entries in her dictionary with the label "G-S," indicating that they appeared in Gatschet and Swanton but could not be verified or remembered by Youchigant. The lack of a Class I intransitive counterpart in this older form lends credence to the hypothesis that the variation was a more recent innovation in Tunica.

The question for KYLY and this lexicographic undertaking was how to treat these verbs moving forward. Is the transitive Tishlina class more authentic because it is the older form? Or is the Class I verb better because it aligns more closely with the learners' experience with active versus passive constructions in English? Those supporting the latter position argued rightly that Class I verbal inflection does not make the verbs less authentic; the roots are still clearly Tunica in origin, and the verbs are inflected according to Tunica grammar. Proponents of Class I labeling also argued that the language would have changed had it been in use for the past sixty years, and Youchigant's forms are evidence that this change would have come to pass. In that sense, Class I inflection is actually *more* authentically Tunica.

However, proponents of linguistic conservatism, those who argued that the older transitive Tishlina form should be the preferred form, were worried about the class shift. Class I verbs are far more frequent in the lexicon; there are only fifty-seven transitive Tishlina verbs, as opposed to 342 Class I verbs. More than half of the transitive Tishlina verbs are listed by Haas as having a possible Class I alternative. Advocates for Tishlina verb class argued that Tishlina verbs bore out an alternate worldview that was inextricably Tunica; Tishlina verbs showcase an unnamed feminine subject that acts on a person, overriding their volition, prompting a person to sweat, cough, or sneeze. If we do not want to erase this unique worldview encoded in the grammar, argued the linguistic conservatives, we should state a strong preference for the Tishlina verb class in these cases.

Ultimately, the proponents of preferentially labeling the verbs as Tishlina prevailed, even though a statistical analysis of the texts showed that Class I intransitive inflection was more common in the *Tunica Texts* (Haas 1950). Again, there is a note in the dictionary saying that Class I intransitive inflection is allowed but that transitive Tishlina inflection is strongly preferred.

Homonymy and Its Influence on Standardization

Given Tunica's reawakening state, there is a strong drive within KYLY to avoid learner confusion. Contemporary Tunica speakers have no native-speaker intuition to rely on, which make homonyms particularly problematic in the early stages of learners' education. It is not surprising, therefore, that when questions of variant standardization arose, the group took into consideration the presence or absence of homonyms. Take, for example, the word *koma*. This word has three distinct senses, each of which Haas lists under separate headwords, as seen in the following example:

> kóma tr. to pick, pluck . . . (a fowl)
> kóma intr. to comb one's hair; tr. to comb. . . . Perh. < Eng.
> > tákóma (agent.) m. a comb
> kóma var. (prob. Incorrect) of kómu
> kómu tr. to sip . . . (e.g., TT 9:f). Var. kóma, prob. incorrect.

Haas does not indicate why she believes the third *koma* to be an incorrect variant of *komu*; in other circumstances this lack of explanation would have caused KYLY to dig into which form it preferred. However, given the presence of two other homonyms, including *koma* 'to comb one's hair', which is a favorite among students because of its similarity to English, KYLY removed the possibly incorrect variant for *komu* 'to sip' from the New Tunica Dictionary.

Homonymity coupled with frequency in Tunica data influenced KYLY's decision in the "standard" form. In the following example, *nohti* was determined to be the standard form based on Haas's description:

> nóhti intr. to rock oneself; tr. to rock. . . . Vars. núhti and núhki, perh.
> > incorrect. In G-S núhti. . c. intr. "to rock oneself," which perh. should
> > be read nóhti. . c.

Nuhki, mentioned by Haas, was disqualified by KYLY as an acceptable variant because it was homonymous with *nuhki* 'otter'. The other listed variant, *nuhti*, was found not in Youchigant's Tunica but in the Gatschet-Swanton cards, meaning that it would not appear in the *Tunica Texts*. Tunica learners are thus unlikely to encounter it in older forms of Tunica. The Gatschet-Swanton materials show wide phonetic variation, even within the same transcribed texts. Variation between /o/ and /u/ is seen elsewhere in these older recorded forms. Therefore, I made the decision to exclude *nuhti* as a headword in the New Tunica Dictionary. A note was included in the FLEx database about this older form, should it interest scholars in the future. However, *nohti* is presented to dictionary users as the sole standard form.

Homonymy also drove the exclusion of what Haas (1953) called "irregular variations" from the dictionary. For *shimu* 'to blow one's nose', Haas notes that it was given as *sihu* and "once as *musha*, the latter perh[aps] < *shimu* with meta[thesis]." *Musha* is also a headword, with the label "irregular variation." *Musha* was something that occurred in Haas's elicitation of one-off sentences; *musha* does not ever appear in the *Tunica Texts*. So while *sihu* was kept in the New Tunica Dictionary as an equivalent of *shimu*, *musha* was excluded entirely. Again, the possibility of a user encountering a variant form in older texts drove this decision. Since *musha* never appeared in older texts, its inclusion in the dictionary would produce clutter with no added value to the user in any real context.

Standardization was a core value of the KYLY, which sought to counteract ambiguity in the interest of easier learning. These values are reflected in how we approached the microstructure of the dictionary. Standardization is not a core value for all groups working on revitalization dictionaries. The dictionary *Chinuk Wawa: kakwa nsayka ulman-tilixam laska munk-kemteks nsayka* (Chinuk Wawa Dictionary Project 2012), for example, has a very different goal: in the front matter, the authors state that their goal is to represent all varieties of the language as speakers actually speak it. To that end, they structure their entries differently, including robust microstructure for more common variations and smaller entries for variants, whose microstructure includes an original source example with name of speaker. Ultimately, the microstructure of the dictionary highlights the core values of its authors. Conscientious effort is required to ensure that these values and language ideologies align with the community that the dictionary is intended to serve.

Macrostructure: Organization of Headwords

Headword Versus Sense

Once you have determined your headwords, it is time to organize them into senses and subsenses. Yet how to divide them? Should *mahka* meaning "expensive" be under the same sense as *mahka* meaning "to love"? What about *muhki,* which can mean "cloud," "to give off smoke," or "to smoke a hide"? Homonymy and polysemy—coexisting meanings for words—pose significant challenges to lexicographers in determining hierarchical organization of headwords. At what point does a meaning merit its own headword, and when is it relegated to a mere subsense of a larger headword? What criteria are used to determine this distinction?

Lexicographers use varied approaches in solving the macrostructural quandaries presented by homonymy and polysemy. One can delineate lemma based on etymology, semantics, or morphology. A historical approach relies heavily on the etymology of a word; a morphosemantic approach favors subentries based on semantics; the formal-grammatical approach determines headwords based strictly on part of speech (Svensén 2009, 96–100). Bo Svensén also points out that lexicographers have been known to mix and match, relying on one approach more heavily than others while cherry-picking word forms that are better represented with different approaches. Each approach has its own set of strengths and weaknesses. For example, lexicographers of learners' dictionaries make several strong arguments for a formal-grammatical approach, in which senses are strictly divided on part of speech (Scholfield 1999; Svensén 2009). This approach is especially useful if the dictionary is intended for reception, as users can often determine a word's part of speech based on its position in a sentence. The division of headwords by part of speech leverages the users' linguistic abilities and leads to more successful lookups (Scholfield 1999). An example of the formal-grammatical approach as applied to the New Tunica Dictionary is seen here:

wɛka₁ *v.T.intr* **1)** get spoiled **2)** get contaminated **3)** get polluted **4)** get defiled
wɛka₂ *adj* **1)** contaminated **2)** polluted **3)** spoiled
wɛka₃ *v.TR.f* **1)** wane (of the moon) **2)** to shine, only used for the moon

Even though *wɛka*₁ and *wɛka*₂ are clearly related etymologically, they are listed as separate headwords given their different word class. This formal-grammatical

Figure 1. Home screen of the New Tunica Dictionary digital app.

approach makes sense in print, and on the home screen of the digital dictionary app, as seen in figure 1. However, this approach tends to isolate information when a word is selected for viewing in the digital app, seen in figure 2. Of course, the digital form also mitigates this sense of isolation, as one can use the arrows at the top of the entry screen to scroll between the different homonyms.

Another possible point of confusion with the formal-grammatical approach is that it can lead to the grouping of semantically unrelated terms under the same

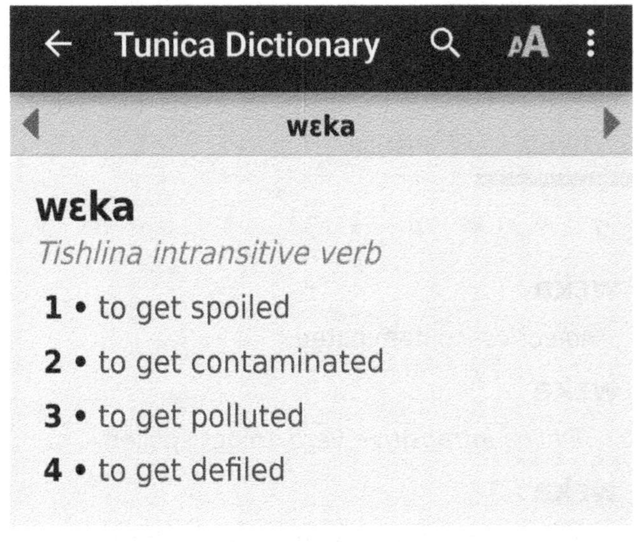

Figure 2. Individual headword view in the New Tunica Dictionary digital app.

headword. For example, the English-language headword "match, *n*" might be followed by the senses (1) game or competition, (2) one who is someone's equal, (3) a possible wife or husband, (4) something that combines well, and (5) a wooden stick for making fire (Svensén 2009, 100). These senses are the same part of speech (noun) but have drastically different meanings.

While the formal-grammatical approach is a valid configuration, I felt that implementing it across the board would be too significant a break from Haas's dictionary and its reliance on semantic headword organization. Though much is changing in the New Tunica Dictionary, KYLY wanted to maintain a connection with the older texts in this macrostructural way. Hence, a mixed semantic and formal-grammatical approach was used to arrange the Tunica data into headwords that were entered into FLEx, resulting in entries delineated first by semantics, and then by part of speech, as seen in the example below.

amari$_1$ *v.II.tr* **1**) to imitate **2**) to mock
amari$_2$ *n* **1**) way **2**) manner
amari$_3$ *v.II.tr* to measure
amari$_4$ *n* a measure, such as an acre

Derived Forms and Suppletive Paradigms

As mentioned earlier in the chapter, another significant deviation in headword choice from Haas's 1953 dictionary is the inclusion of complete suppletive verbal paradigms as distinct headwords. Tunica auxiliary verbs (called *lupirani* 'chameleon' verbs) are highly suppletive; they follow irregular inflection patterns (like *to go* in English). For convenience, Haas (1940, 41) arbitrarily chose the third-person masculine singular form as the reference form. So for example, for the verb *una* 'he sits, sat', Haas (1953) lists only this one form and then includes in the entry a reference to her Tunica grammar (Haas 1940). A user would need to consult this other text to find the verb's other forms (*anani, wina, hɛna, achi, uk'ɛra*, etc.), which are completely unlisted in the 1953 dictionary.

Given that these auxiliary verb forms cannot be intuited through regular Tunica morphological processes, I felt that it was important to include all forms as independent headwords in the New Tunica Dictionary. When a user encounters the word *itashi* in a text or conversation, it is unrealistic to expect him to derive and look up the third-person masculine singular form, *uwa*. A one-to-one relationship between what the dictionary user expects and what he finds in the dictionary is crucial in these cases and ensures a high level of overall dictionary usability.

Alphabetical Versus Semantic Order

The ordering of headwords is a question that largely pertains to print dictionaries. Digital dictionaries are rarely browsed from start to finish, and a search box is the most common way that a user finds headwords in a digital dictionary, making ordering a moot point. Given that the New Tunica Dictionary will appear in print form, ordering was discussed; KYLY initially planned to make the New Tunica Dictionary strictly alphabetical. This choice was a departure from Haas (1953), who, as seen with the *hayi* example earlier in this chapter, made ample use of nesting, which resulted in nonalphabetical ordering. A regular complaint raised when using the Haas dictionary is that one has to know the morphology of a word in order to find the word. However, while observing Tunica learners use the dictionary app, I noticed them performing several interesting searches that would have been difficult to replicate in a strictly alphabetical print dictionary format. For example, one student wanted to know all the different kinds of traditional dances found in the Tunica dictionary. A search for the word *dance* in the app returned all headwords with this word anywhere in the entry, such as *Yishihipu* 'Raccoon Dance' and *Lawutɛhkalahipu* 'Midnight Dance'. This speaker's search intrigued me; he was using the dictionary not to access a definition but to inventory an aspect of Tunica culture. It prompted me to ask how we could facilitate similar searches in a print dictionary.

Consensus among KYLY was to nest certain cultural vocabulary under generic headwords on the English–Tunica side only. The resulting entry for *dance* is as follows:

dance *n* hipu, nihkirhipu *Tarushtaku, "Nihkirhipu yahkarani hɛlawu,"*
nikɔni. Rabbit said, "I'm giving a ball tonight," they say. *"Tosinlupiku*
tanihkirhipuhch yakaw'ihch, lapuhch," nikɔni. "If Whooping Crane
were to come to the ball, it would be a good thing," he said, they say.
Tahch'ahipuhch, Yoroni-Halayihku sihknihkirhipu yuk'aki. The Tunica-
Biloxi Pow-Wow comes in May.
Alligator Dance Ɔmahkahipu
Bear Dance Nokushhipu
Chicken Dance Kapashhipu
Commencement of Midnight Dance Tirishchɔhatawɛsa
Daybreak Dance Lawu Aharahipu
Double-Head Dance Osin'ilihipu
Duck Dance Kuwahipu
Fox Dance Chulahipu
Horse Dance Sat'ɛhipu
Mallard Duck Dance Tɔhkat'ɛhipu
Midnight Dance Lawutɛhkalahipu
Pumpkin Dance Shulihkhipu
Quail Dance Hikihipu
Rabbit Dance Rushtahipu
Raccoon Dance Yishihipu
Round Dance Tirishchɔhahipu
Sheep Dance Rushtat'ɛhipu
Skunk Dance Shikihipu
Snake Dance Narahipu

Turtle Dance Kohkuhipu
War Dance Tirishchɔhahipu
Wood Tick Dance Sa'ɔnanhipu

Each of the dance types nested under the headword also appears as its own headword in the alphabetically expected location. Those standalone entries have a more robust microstructure, including example sentences that describe specific aspects of the dance.

This nesting strategy is limited to a handful of headwords of cultural significance, such as stickball and regalia. Given that these cultural practices are being revitalized alongside the language, I felt it important to reference them centrally so that dictionary users might have all the vocabulary they need to participate in the activity and produce Tunica. KYLY has discussed expanding this practice into other domains such as plants and animals—there are nine different species of oak trees listed in the dictionary—or even days of the week, codifying lexicographic nesting as a pedagogic tool. However, such nesting takes up more space since the headwords are duplicated. Given the increased cost of printing, I advised that KYLY pilot samples of the different printed formats with users to determine whether nesting these more generic topics resulted in a better dictionary experience or better language retention.

To meet their current pedagogic needs, Tunica teachers have used FLEx to record semantic domain for all headwords in the database. This semantic designation does not flow to the dictionary, but it does allow Tunica teachers to easily create language lessons; if they are teaching a lesson on weather, for example, they can easily poll FLEx for the information. This additional metadata has also prompted conversations about publishing various quick guides to the language based on semantic domain. While this task is yet to be realized, the work done while entering lexicographic information into FLEx makes it easy for the data to be reused in nonalphabetical ways in future reference works.

Megastructure

Megastructure is a broad term referring to everything in the dictionary that is not related to individual headwords or headword organization. It can include front matter, back matter, and general ordering of languages in multilingual dictionaries. The front matter of the New Tunica Dictionary includes an introduction in Tunica and English, a history of the language revitalization project, and a sketch grammar of the language. As of 2020, this sketch grammar is one of only two complete grammar references available to learners of modern Tunica, the other being a beginning language textbook (KYLY forthcoming). The multifunctional design of the New Tunica Dictionary is driven by user need, bringing it into the realm of functional lexicography. For easy access, the back matter or appendices of the New Tunica Dictionary include helpful quick references to common irregular verbal paradigms. In contrast, Haas uses her front matter to open up a discussion of her work on the "linguistic affiliations" in Tunica and borrowings into Tunica. She also uses the front matter to describe her Tunica sources at length. Haas does not include any back matter in her 1953 dictionary.

The front and back matter in dictionaries can be designed in a wide variety of ways to meet lexicographers' goals or users' needs. In other Indigenous-language dictionaries, I have seen front matter that contains everything from maps, to extensive accounts of language history, to minibiographies of the speakers who contributed. While the design and execution of the New Tunica Dictionary's front and back matter did not engender much debate, another aspect of the dictionary's macrostructure, language order, gave KYLY pause.

Tunica–English and English–Tunica: Order and Legitimacy in the Dictionary

While a bilingual dictionary can be unidirectional—with words from language A glossed in language B but not the reverse—the expectation of modern bilingual dictionaries is that they are bidirectional. A fundamental question of a bilingual dictionary's macrostructure is which language appears first. Most lexicographers argue that the ordering of languages very much depends on the kinds of linguistic activity the user will be undertaking (Svensén 2009; Sterkenburg 2003). If the user is going from their native L1 to their acquired L2, consequently using the dictionary for L2 production, then their native language should be listed first. Conversely, if the dictionary is for reception, the L2–L1 half should come first. Functional lexicography seconds this argument, stating that prioritizing the language of operation gives user easier access and leads to quicker, more successful lookups (Rundell 1999; Scholfield 1999).

As there are no native speakers of Tunica, the L1 language of all users of the New Tunica Dictionary will be English. Furthermore, Tunica learners are being encouraged to produce Tunica in their homes and in the classroom, meaning that their primary motivation in using the dictionary will be active language production, going from their L1 (English) to their L2 (Tunica). From a pure frequency-of-use standpoint, the English–Tunica side will be referenced most often. In theory, quick and accurate lookups result in users returning to the dictionary for future queries. Given that the TLP seeks to promote widespread production of the Tunica language in all domains, one can make the argument that placing the English–Tunica side of the dictionary first is the most practical choice.

However, as we have seen, dictionaries are not a neutral compilation of words and definitions, and the ways in which they are structured have a tangible impact on the way in which users and outside nonusers see a language. Just as the mere existence of a Tunica dictionary gives the language legitimacy, so too does the hierarchy of languages within a bilingual dictionary convey authority. Placing Tunica–English first gives weight and authority to the Tunica language. Ultimately, KYLY decided that it preferred the Tunica–English side to be first in the printed dictionary and on screen in the digital versions. The consensus was that the legitimacy and prestige bestowed on Tunica—a reawakening language—by placing the Tunica–English side first outweighed the potential downsides of usability. Indeed, requiring users to flip through the Tunica–English side on their way to English–Tunica has the added bonus of serendipity. Lexicographer Erin McKean (2007) describes serendipity as "when you find things you weren't looking for, because finding what you are looking for is so damned difficult." In the case of Tunica, lexicographic serendipity brings words to users' attention that they may not have found otherwise, as they did not even know such words existed. This is especially true of words that do not have English equivalence, such as *pɔk*, an imitative word of the sound a rabbit makes. It is the hope of KYLY that these words will take on new meaning and life in a new cultural context. These dual factors of legitimacy and serendipity resulted in the intentional placement of the Tunica–English side of the dictionary first, making it a user's entry point for both print and digital versions.

A Wrap on Dictionary Structure

No part of a dictionary "just happens" or is inevitable. All aspects of lexicographic organization are decisions or assumptions made by the human lexicographers behind the project. All dictionaries of all languages are the sum of lexicographer goals, user needs, and unspoken assumptions about what constitutes dictionary structure. It is my hope that this chapter has given other lexicographers and dictionary makers the tools needed to evaluate a dictionary's structure, from the micro to the macro. Given that few minority-language projects have the resources they would like to fully develop all components of dictionary structure, it is useful to clearly align resource allocation and lexicographic goals. Community collaboration in designing the dictionary's structure and organization helps ensure that the dictionary will be usable to and accepted by generations of new language speakers.

Chapter Five

Neologisms and the Dictionary

[Building the dictionary] has made me think more about how we want to express concepts that did not exist in Sesostrie's time, of course.

—BRENDA LINTINGER
Tunica-Biloxi councilwoman

New words are a hallmark of any living language, a sign that speakers are willing to invest energy and resources in a language's longevity. Lexicographers have long grappled with how to approach new words in the dictionary. How soon is too soon to include new language? Does including new language devalue or add value to a dictionary? The legacy of dictionaries as authoritative objects coupled with the dictionary compilers' language ideology will influence the threshold of new word inclusion. However, a revitalization approach to lexicography adds a consideration; if the revitalization process entails creating new words to expand the language into new domains, how does the dictionary support this project? What elements of dictionary making can be leveraged to facilitate meaningful new word creation?

New words, also known as neologisms, can be formed through any number of grammatically sound methods, such as compounding (thanks + giving = Thanksgiving) and back-formation (editor − or = edit). Regardless of how new words come to be, neologisms give speakers access to nuances of meaning and means of expression that evolve as quickly as the world around us. *Photobomb* and *binge-watch*, for example, have been in use for less than two decades.[1] The importance

---

1. The first recorded use of *photobomb* was in 2008. It is recognized as a word by both *Merriam-Webster* and the *Oxford English Dictionary*. *Binge-watch* is older, first seen in 2003; *Merriam-Webster* includes it as a word, but the *Oxford English Dictionary* does not.

of acknowledging lexical innovation is not lost on lexicographers. Most modern English-language dictionaries widely publicize a yearly update of their lexicon, such as *Merriam-Webster*'s announcement in 2017 that it was adding one thousand words to the dictionary. A contemporary dictionary that does not stay up to date risks becoming obsolete.

However, lexicographers have not always been so keen on adding new words. As discussed in chapter 2, dictionaries have historically been held up as curators and protectors of a language. New words, especially those created by younger speakers, can be portrayed as a threat to a language, jeopardizing its organization and purity. A dictionary that adds neologisms too hastily could be construed as falling down on its gatekeeping responsibilities or, worse, encouraging young speakers in their ruinous use of language. Perhaps that is why *baked potato* and *coffee maker* were not added to the *Oxford English Dictionary* until 2014. Oxford Dictionaries, until very recently, would not publish any word that had been in print less than two years (Oxford Dictionaries 2014), though as a stopgap measure, the *Oxford English Dictionary* (n.d.a.) has created a category dubbed "nonwords" for documented language that has insufficient "legitimate" usage. However, the continued shift toward descriptivism and the incredible popularity of dictionaries like UrbanDictionary.com have convinced larger publishing houses to modify their new word practices. Not only have dictionaries moved up their timeline on publication, they have also created digital storehouses for user-reported words that merit investigation. *Merriam-Webster*'s Open Dictionary is an online public repository of neologisms and slang that may eventually make it into the unabridged published dictionary. *Collins Dictionary* solicits user submissions as well. Though there is still gatekeeping and language "quality control" in these larger dictionaries, they have opened a path for quicker inclusion of new words.

Neologisms are also a significant topic in language revitalization. Once these words are created, language revitalization lexicographers have to decide what to do with them. How quickly should new words be added to the dictionary? What are the criteria for including a new word versus excluding it? The answers to these questions differ from community to community based on the factors that are motivating neologism creation; for example, neologisms that fill gaps in the

---

Merriam-Webster, s.v. "photobomb," s.v. "binge-watch," accessed December 19, 2017, https://www.merriam-webster.com/; *Oxford English Dictionary*, s.v. "photobomb," accessed December 30, 2017, http://www.oed.com/.

language may be more readily included than neologisms that are replacing older counterparts. Neologisms that are created by motivated young speakers may be rejected from the dictionary because they are not "authentic," or they may be included more readily to document the meaning for older speakers and reward youngsters for their creativity. Decisions to include neologisms may also be influenced by the kind of dictionary being made; an unabridged dictionary of the entire history and future of a language may readily publish new words, whereas a dictionary meant to be used in the classroom as an educator-approved textbook may exclude them. A dictionary of scientific and technical language will likely be filled with neologisms since words such as *isosceles triangle* were likely not recorded historically, whereas a dictionary based solely on published historical documents may be more restrictive.

With the New Tunica Dictionary, I found that the decisions to include or exclude neologisms were not uniform. The Tunica language community deemed certain neologisms more acceptable and therefore worthy of inclusion in the dictionary, while others were put on the back burner to await further evidence of use. This chapter explores who is creating Tunica neologisms, why they are being created, and what that means for the New Tunica Dictionary.

What Drives Tunica Neologism Creation?

From the outset of the Tunica language revitalization effort, it was clear that the creation of neologisms would be essential to the process of bringing Tunica into everyday use. Many lexical domains are underrepresented or completely lacking in historical documented Tunica. The reasons for these gaps are multifold. Obviously, technologies have changed rapidly since Sesostrie Youchigant died in 1948, and there are no documented Tunica words for items that did not exist at that time, such as telephones, computers, or roller skates. But there were also words that were doubtlessly part of the Tunica lexical inventory when it was a robust living language; unfortunately, these words were not recorded by scholars or were not remembered by the language's last speakers. In some cases, the scholar may have failed to ask about a certain domain. But most lexical gaps of this nature derive form the precarious state of the Tunica language at the time of its recording. As is frequent with last speakers of endangered languages, Youchigant had not had anyone to converse with in Tunica for nearly twenty years at the time of his work with Mary R. Haas. In one instance, Haas (n.d.a., 8:103) writes in her field notebooks that Youchigant said previous generations used to know the Tunica month and day names, but that he could not recall them. These gaps must be filled with neologisms.

As the language continues to awaken, Tunica speakers find that they want to say things that never existed in historical Tunica as a direct translation. Politeness terms such as *please, thank you,* and *excuse me* are important to native English speakers, even though politeness would not necessarily have taken this form in older Tunica; consequently *tikahch* 'thank you' (lit. "it would be a big thing") was the very first neologism created as part of revitalization. Other words such as *birthday* and *weekend* represent Eurocentric concepts that contemporary Tunica speakers nonetheless want to express. The goal of the Tunica Language Project (TLP) is to create a living language that allows speakers to use Tunica in any domain. Accordingly, all domains encountered by modern Tunica speakers require Tunica expressions.

Most Tunica neologisms have been created by the Tunica working group (Kuhpani Yoyani Luhchi Yoroni, KYLY). Indeed, neologisms are a regular topic of conversation in KYLY's weekly meetings. Language teachers translating "Frosty the Snowman" into Tunica need a word for *snowman*. Students compiling a pamphlet on Tunica medicinal plants want an equivalent for the phrase "scientific name" in Tunica. New words created by the group are inputted into the Tunica database, with notes about the circumstances of their creation. However, KYLY is not the only contributor of new words, as we shall see later in the chapter. Regardless of who makes words or how, the consensus among those working on the TLP is that the dictionary should document the language as it is spoken, and that neologisms should not be stigmatized for future Tunica speakers.

New Tunica Words in Old Tunica Dictionaries

New words were recorded in the earliest Tunica documents, demonstrating that Tunica, like any other living language, evolves with the needs of the speakers. Haas, of course, was the most systematic in marking words that she or Youchigant considered to be not native to Tunica. The Haas data shows that Tunica employs many of the same strategies used by other Indigenous languages when incorporating new words, such as language-internal word constructions, borrowings, and semantic extension (Denzer-King 2008; Davis 2018). Haas uses different conventions to denote these different speaker strategies in her 1953 dictionary. Borrowings are indicated by clearly marking in a word's dictionary entry the language from which it was borrowed: *huraka* 'hurricane' from Spanish *huracán*, *tini* 'to eat dinner' from French *dîner*, and *chula* 'fox' from Choctaw *chula*. Haas also makes note of claques, or translation borrowings. For example, Tunica is *owita'ira* 'sweater' is a literal translation of "sweat-clother." *Chuhkirisa* is a literal translation of "gray oak." Translated idioms are also labeled by Haas, such as *tetit'ɛhchi chu* or "take the highway." Haas notes that this phrase involves an idiomatic use of the Tunica verb *chu* 'to take, get, or obtain' that mirrors a literal English translation, but that the word is not used in this way in other language contexts. In all these examples, Haas explicitly calls out the fact that these words are neologisms of borrowed origin.

Neologisms that are created from purely Tunica words via compounding are not explicitly marked as such by Haas. However, they are given extra attention. For example, next to *ahkalayihtatahinu* 'train', Haas writes "lit. smoke-on-the-level"; and next to *onrɔwahka* 'rice' appears "lit. white man's corn." Given their content, these entries are clearly new Tunica. Words for train and rice would not have been present in the language two hundred years prior. The extralinguistic information about literal translations clearly delineates these words as neologisms. From their special treatment, we know that Haas was keenly aware of neologisms in Tunica and felt it important that users of her *Tunica Dictionary* be aware of them too.

The New Tunica Dictionary departs from Haas's *Tunica Dictionary* in a number of ways (Anderson 2017), but one of the most significant and intentional departures is the treatment of neologisms. The lexical database that feeds the New Tunica Dictionary marks new words as neologisms, recording approximate date of creation and noting the context of where it was first seen. However, this information does *not* flow into the published dictionary. The information is available to researchers or especially curious language learners providing they have access to the shared FLEx database. But the dictionary user is not burdened with this information. The decision to keep such labels out of the dictionary was deliberate, an attempt to foster acceptance of new words. Neologisms are essential to the continued expansion and revitalization of the Tunica language, and KYLY feared that labeling these words would stigmatize them in some way. The TLP expressed a strong desire for Tunica speakers to see neologisms as equally authentic to older Tunica words. To that end, the information is safely tucked away in the database, so it is accessible for future research, but withheld from print to discourage the delegitimization of neologisms.

Strategies for Neologism Creation in Tunica

Many factors inspire the creation of Tunica neologisms. Primary motivations for new word creation include: the needs of Tunica teachers for lessons and classroom management; the desire of the Tribe to make Tunica more visible in the community; the creation of technical Tunica resources such as a textbook and the dictionary; and the creativity encouraged during the annual Tunica summer camp. The Tunica language has several innate strategies that allow speakers to communicate new and complex ideas. Every strategy presented below is documented in older Tunica materials unless explicitly noted as an exception. The exceptions are very few, as Tunica has robust compounding mechanisms, resulting in highly descriptive and nuanced language. As lexicographer, I had to stay in touch with the creations of new Tunica speakers and the Tunica working group; both are prolific, adding new words to the Tunica lexicon on a regular basis. In addition to utilizing the strategies already present in Tunica, KYLY also innovated new processes to ensure that neologisms be succinct enough for everyday use. To demonstrate the robustness of Tunica word creation, I outline the most common and productive strategies in this section. All words presented are neologisms, added to the Tunica lexicon as part of the revitalization process.

New Nouns

Nouns can be derived from Class I and Class II verbs. In the case of Class I verbs, no marker is needed to indicate that the new word is a noun. This lack of marker is also known as zero derivation.

> *niyu* 'idea'—from *niyu* v.I.intr 'to think, believe'
> *luwa* 'mixture'—from *luwa* v.I.tr 'to mix, stir in, dilute'
> *haha* 'curse'—from *haha* v.I.tr 'to curse'

When a Class II verb is used to build the new word, the suffix *-ni* is required to turn it into a noun.

> *wisani* 'joke'—from *wisa* v.II.tr 'to play a joke or trick on'
> *arhilani* 'story'—from *arhila* v.II.intr 'to tell a story'

woruni 'example'—from *woru* v.II.tr 'to teach'
palani 'bingo!'—from *pala* v.II.tr 'to cause to win in gambling'

If a verb has both Class I and Class II forms, the presence or absence of *-ni* gives nuances of meaning.

kipa 'marriage'—from *kipa* v.I.tr 'to marry'
kipani 'arranged marriage'—from *kipa* v.II.tr 'to marry off'

Adding the agentive *ta-* to Tunica verbs has also resulted in many neologisms. Agentive *ta-* is equivalent to the *-er* suffix in English. Teacher means one who teachers, and washer means one who washes. *Ta-* appears in such neologisms as the following:

takɛra 'farmer'—from *kɛra* v.I.intr 'to scatter seed'
tahapa 'quitter'—from *hapa* v.I.intr 'to stop, quit'

New Adjectives

Adjectives are zero derived. Unlike nouns, the class of the verb does not matter when forming adjectives. The following examples are found in Haas (1953):

pɛlka 'flat'—from *pɛlka* v.II.tr 'to flatten'
lepu 'bent'—from *lepu* v.I.intr 'to bend'

Compounding

NOUN + ADJECTIVE COMPOUNDS

Noun + adjective compounds result in new nouns. The adjective provides description that can then be extrapolated for a new nominal meaning. Contemporary Tunica speakers have made several neologisms using this strategy, as follows:

tetimili 'culture'—from *teti* 'path' + *mili* 'red'
ashutayi 'week'—from *ashu* 'day' + *tayi* 'seven'
ashutɛhkala 'noon'—from *ashu* 'day' + *tɛhkala* 'middle'

NOUN + NOUN COMPOUNDS

Noun + noun compounds result in an entirely new noun. In noun + noun constructions, the descriptive noun is always first, followed by the determining noun.

pirashu 'birthday' — from *pira* 'birth' + *ashu* 'day'
kosuwishi 'paint' — from *kosu* 'color' + *wishi* 'water'

If one of the nouns is formed using the agentive *ta-*, the agentive noun is second.

ritarapu 'hotel' — from *ri* 'house' + *tarapu* 'sleeper'

NOUN + VERB COMPOUNDS

Noun + verb compounds create new nouns. If the verb is Class II, the suffix *-ni* is required to make a noun.

takashimi 'toy' — *taka* 'thing' + *shimi* 'to play'
takayuwa 'gift' — *taka* 'thing' + *yuwa* 'to present with something'
sat'ɛhɛsani 'saw-horse' — *sat'ɛ* 'horse' + *hɛsa* 'to saw' v.II + *-ni*

VERB + VERB COMPOUNDS

In documented Tunica, verbs can be compounded, giving rise to a new, more nuanced meaning. Examples from older Haas (1953; n.d.a., 8:165) data include:

poyaka 'to court' — from *po* + *yaka* — lit. "to come and see"
tapiheni 'to shake hands' — from *tapi* + *heni* — lit. "to grab and greet"

Following this pattern, KYLY created the following:

kɔwawɛla 'to carve' — from *kɔwa* + *wɛla* — lit. "to pare and cut"

Affixation

Another strategy uses widespread Tunica word endings, or affixes, to build complete word forms.

tikahch 'thank you'—from *tika* + *-hch*—lit. "it was a big thing"
tohkuhch 'please'—from *tohku* + *-hch*—lit. "it would be a small thing"
kɔrashi 'garage'—from *kɔra* + *-shi*—lit. "place of the car"
hɛrashi 'waiting'—from *hɛra* + *-shi*—lit. "place to wait"

Use of Directional Prefixes

The prefixes *ha-*, *ho-*, *lu-*, and *ki-* are very productive in Tunica. These prefixes indicate a sense of directionality, such as whether an action takes place in a vertical plane or in a horizontal direction. These prefixes have been applied to a limited set of neologisms, seen below.

hahpu 'to shower'—from *ha-* + *ahpu*—lit. "to bathe in a vertical position"
lulɔsa 'to download'—from *lu-* + *lɔsa*—lit. "to pull downward"

In Haas (1953), these prefixes can only be used with verbs. However, KYLY has expanded their use, prepending them to nouns as well.

hawishi 'straw'—from *ha-* + *wishi*—lit. "vertical liquid"
luwishi 'downspout'—from *lu-* + *wishi*—lit. "downward liquid"

Semantic Extension and Specialization

Several neologisms extend or narrow the semantic qualities of Tunica words, based on their English gloss. In this sense, the semantic relations are borrowed from English and then applied to Tunica.

heni 'hello'—from *heni* v.I.tr 'to greet'
rasht'ɛ 'difficult, hard'—from *rasht'ɛ* adv. 'with great effort'
hinu 'to exercise'—from *hinu* v.I.intr 'to bustle about'
eri 'to upload'—from *eri* v.I.tr 'to lift, hoist, raise up'
kolu 'to subtract'—from *kolu* v.I.tr 'to snatch away from'
sara 'sorry!'—from *sara* v.I.tr 'to beg, implore'
tishtahpu 'Facebook'—from *ti* + *shtahpu* 'her face'

In addition to extending and narrowing the meanings of single-word roots, KYLY has analyzed compound words and extended or narrowed the meaning of the roots in order to create neologisms. In compound forms, roots often have variation in meaning not seen when they stand on their own. This variation gives speakers more room for linguistic creativity. For example, *uma* is the neologism for "animal," derived from the documented word *yorum'aha* 'wild beast'. *Yoruma* is not documented on its own, which gave the creators a choice in interpretation. Was the root *yoruma* or *yoru* + *uma*? The latter seemed more "Tunica," with its two canonical disyllabic roots.[2] *Uma* was adopted as "animal," and *yoru* was placed on the back burner as a possible future neologism should the need arise.

In another instance, the Tunica teachers needed a general term for "color." While several specific terms for colors were recorded (such as *kayi* 'yellow', *mili* 'red', and *risa* 'variegated'), no word for the overall concept was written down. In a brainstorming session, KYLY members agreed that rainbows consisted of many colors and therefore would be a candidate for the neologism. However, the three words recorded by Haas (1953) for rainbow are all quite long: *kosuyuwishi, kosuwihu,* and *kosuhk'ariya.* Their common element, *kosu,* is derived from *kosuhki,* the word for crawfish; the Crawfish Shaman, responsible for whirlwinds that sucked up crawfish, was said to have a rainbow painted on his face, which could be seen following such events. The group opted to adopt *kosu* as the word for color, extending the word beyond its original reference to the tasty crustacean.

Metonymy and Synecdoche

Documented Tunica presents us with many examples of metonymy. English uses this strategy widely as well, as for example when British royalty is referred to as the Crown. In historical Tunica, terms relating to Christianity contain the word *meli* 'black' because Catholic priests dressed in all black. Words such as *Ashumeli* 'Easter' (lit. "black day") and *kapash'ohkumeli* 'Easter egg' (lit. "black egg") demonstrate *meli*'s use. The Tunica word for priest is *mel'ira* (lit. "black clothed").

---

2. Haas documented all words as CVCV (consonant-vowel-consonant-vowel), with an initial glottal when no other consonant is present. Standardized Tunica has done away with writing nonphonemic glottal stops. But in this way, it can be argued that *uma* has an underlying CVCV structure.

It is conceivable that *meli* on its own was used to refer to priests, hence its use in other contexts that are closely associated with priests.[3] Other associations in historical Tunica are likely derived via synecdoche, a figure of speech in which an object is referenced by calling attention to a part of it. In Tunica, *rihkɔra* 'wagon' is composed of the lexemes *rihku* and *kɔra*; *rihkɔra* literally means "disc-shaped wood." Haas (1950, 249) notes that this word likely refers to the wagon's wheels.

KYLY has employed both metonymy and synecdoche in creating neologisms. *Kɔra* as a noun has been adopted to mean "car." This new definition of *kɔra* is listed in the dictionary alongside its previously documented senses (the adjective "disc-shaped" and the noun "wheel"). *Pahi* was derived from the noun *pahita* 'lightning'. It is used to denote anything that is lightning fast or electric. Using *pahi*, we get the following neologisms:

pahitahina	'keyboard'	*pahi + tahina*	lit. "electric writer"
pahitaniyu	'computer'	*pahi + taniyu*	lit. "electric thinker"
pahitaniy'ɛsa	'tablet, iPad'	*pahi + taniyu + ɛsa*	lit. "flat electric thinker"
pahitaniyutohku	'laptop'	*pahi + taniyu + -tohku*	lit. "small electric thinker"
pahitawali	'telephone'	*pahi + tawali*	lit. "electric caller"
pahitawira	'calculator'	*pahi + tawira*	lit. "electric counter"
halanipahi	'television'	*halani + pahi*	lit. "electric picture"

Pahi is glossed as an adjective; indeed, it is listed as a headword in the new dictionary as an adjective meaning "digital, electric." However, as we see in the examples above, it usually compounds as if it were a noun. Just as *rowinatahina* 'pencil' is most literally glossed as "writer that uses paper as its medium," not as a "paper writer," so too would *pahitaniyu* most literally be "a thinker that uses electricity to accomplish its task." *Halanipahi* is the exception, with *pahi* compounding in the way that adjectives are expected to compound.

Mimicking Patterns Present in Tunica

Neologisms can be formed by mimicking patterns present in documented Tunica. The most notable uses of this strategy are exemplified in KYLY's treatment of

---

3. Contemporary Tunica leaners are hesitant to use *meli* in its historical sense for Christianity. They have already made several neologisms that eschew this association, such as *esinɛra* 'godparent' (lit. "spirit parent").

interrogatives. Interrogatives as documented by scholars consist of the following words:

kaku 'who'
kata 'where'
kashku 'how many'
ka'ash 'when'
kanahku 'what, what kind, why, in what way, how'

The last word, *kanahku*, frustrated both teachers and learners alike for its broad scope. English has clear delineations between what, how, and why. Tunica speakers repeatedly expressed the desire for an interrogative system that followed English more closely.

KYLY quickly assigned the gloss "how" to *kana*,[4] a shortened form found in documented Tunica that was synonymous with *kanahku*. But "why" was still an issue. During one of the grammar intensives in KYLY's 2015 immersion workshop, the group tackled the lingering interrogative. Upon further analysis, it was concluded that three of the documented interrogatives can be clearly identified as composites of an unidentified stem *ka* with various affixation.

kaku 'who' — from *ka* + *-ku* 'he'
ka'ash 'when' — from *ka* + *ash*, likely derived from *ashu* 'day'
kanahku 'what, why, how' — from *ka* + *-nahku* 'like, resembling'

Following this pattern, the group decided on the neologism *kaya* for "why." *Kaya* is a composite of *ka* + *ya* 'to do, to happen to, to become of a certain quality'.

In that same session, KYLY members decided to liberate *shku* of *kashku* 'how many'. The decision to adopt *kaya* formalized the group's acceptance that the interrogative was productive; it seemed logical to extend this principle to the formerly lexicalized *kashku*, deeming it a composite of *ka* + *-shku*. As it happened, mathematics was still lacking a term for "equals, totals." *Shku* was

---

4. Some in KYLY have regretted this decision, as *kana* has many homonyms, including "something, anything," "to step, to pace," and "a step." It is possible that *kana* meaning "how" will be dropped for another construction in the future.

designated a stative verb, and "equals, totals" of mathematical equations would be *sihkshku*.[5]

An official translation has not been given to the stem *ka*, and it does not appear as an independent headword in the New Tunica Dictionary. However, the word *taka* 'thing' was created using the articular *ta-* + *ka*.

Antonymic Verbs

Strategies to create neologisms presented thus far were all documented by Haas in Youchigant's Tunica and are comprehensive in their ability to create new nouns and adjectives. However, documented Tunica did not provide many strategies for the creation of new verbs. This omission presented a problem for certain verbs that have no documented antonyms. For example, *lahpi* is a Class I verb that means "to put on one's shoes." But there is no documented verb for "to take off one's shoes." When KYLY encountered adjectives without antonyms, the problem could be easily resolved through negation: *pusa* 'polite' could become its opposite, "rude," by adding *-'aha* to form *pus'aha* (lit. "not polite"). But this strategy does not work for verbs. "He did not put on his shoes" is not equivalent to "he took off his shoes."

To fill this lacuna, KYLY adopted consonantal metathesis, or the swapping of two consonants in a word to create a new word.[6] From *huchi* 'to put on a robe', KYLY derived the neologism *chuhi* 'to take off a robe'. In the same vein, *wohku* 'to put on a hat' and *lahpi* 'to put on one's shoes' have new counterparts, *kowu* 'to take off one's hat' and *pali* 'to take off one's shoes'. These examples show that pre-aspirated consonants lose their aspiration when they undergo metathesis.

Building on this strategy, KYLY has also used consonantal metathesis as a productive process with other parts of speech. From the example seen earlier, a

---

5. In retrospect, this decision was somewhat dubious from a grammatical standpoint. There are no other examples of stative verbs taking a non-pronominal affix, such as *ka-*, or even of stative verbs joining with another verb stem. The existence of the documented *kashku* opens the door to questions about permitted behaviors of stative verbs. However, Tunica learners have not raised concerns about this construction to date. If they do ever query it, the explanation offered may be that the older form *kashku* is fossilized and therefore irregular.

6. Consonantal metathesis was chosen over syllabic metathesis because Tunica words can only end in /a/, /i/, or /u/. Moving entire syllables would break this rule in certain words. For example, *wohku* 'to put on a hat' cannot undergo syllabic metathesis because it forms **kuwo*, a word ending in a forbidden /o/.

neologism for "rude" is *supa* (instead of the longer *pus'aha*). This option shortens the word and gives it a canonical disyllabic CVCV (consonant-vowel-consonant-vowel) structure, effectively making it more authentically Tunica. Stative verbs have been created using this strategy as well. For example, *p'ɛsha* 'to be sad' was created via the consonantal metathesis of *sh'ɛpa* 'to be happy'.

In addition to providing verbal antonyms, consonantal metathesis has been employed to disambiguate meaning. For example, the verb *lapu* historically meant "to trade, barter, buy, or sell." This meaning makes sense at the time of Tunica's recording; before widespread currency, buying and selling were not the distinct concepts they are today. An exchange of goods was bidirectional and therefore only needed one word. However, as native speakers of English in contemporary society, Tunica speakers clearly delineate between buying and selling. KYLY decided that *lapu* would keep its bidirectional meaning, glossed as "to trade or barter." The meanings of "to buy" and "to sell" were relegated to a new word, *palu*. A product of consonantal metathesis, *palu* as a Class I verb means "to buy" and as a Class II verb means "to sell."

Calques

Documented Tunica has examples of calques, or words formed as a direct translation, such as the aforementioned *owita'ira* 'sweater'. No neologisms have yet been created using borrowed or idiomatic calques, although this strategy could be employed moving forward. Documented examples are generally toponyms or foodstuffs:

> *tarirɔwa* 'Washington, D.C.'—lit. "the white house"
> *tuhrat'ɛ* 'Grand Ile'—lit. "big island"
> *yanishitihki* 'Bayou Boeuf'—lit. "bovine bayou"
> *yashikayi* 'yellow fever'—lit. "yellow fever/sickness"
> *yit'ɛwista* 'sweet potato'—lit. "sweet marsh potato"
> *alahahchuwista* 'sugar cane'—lit. "salt sweet cane"

Borrowing

Documented Tunica has many examples of borrowing from neighboring Native American languages and from European-contact languages. Haas makes explicit note of these borrowings (1946, 1950). Documented examples include the following:

paska 'Pascagoula Indian'—from Mobilian or Choctaw
huraka 'hurricane'—from Spanish *huracán*
disu 'dime'—from French *dix sous*

Contemporary Tunica borrowings use English as the source language:

fihch 'finch'
penku 'penguin'

Borrowing is KYLY's least favored strategy. The group makes every attempt to use one of the other processes before resorting to borrowing. However, *penku* was submitted by a Tunica language learner independent of KYLY. The trend of borrowing is worth further study as the language is adopted and adapted by new Tunica speakers.

Out with the Old, In with the New

The general approach of KYLY to the creation of neologisms has been to fill in gaps where the language is lacking, rather than to replace historical words recorded by previous scholars. However, in some domains, there was a glaring necessity to rewrite recorded Tunica word forms. The replaced words generally fell under the category of divisions of time: days of the week, months of the year, and so forth. Words for days and months were recorded by previous scholars, but their elicitation methods were dubious. For example, the seven days of the week recorded by the earliest linguists roughly translate into "big day" (Sunday), "one sleep after the big day" (Monday), "two sleeps after the big day" (Tuesday), and so on. The pattern continues until Saturday, *samdi*, which is a direct borrowing from French. Youchigant rejected all day names recorded by Albert S. Gatschet and John R. Swanton, with the exception of Saturday and Sunday (Haas 1953, s.v. "ɁašutɁɛ").

Elicitations about time are suspect because of the high likelihood that European outsiders and Tunica speakers had different divisions of time. The Tunica people most likely did not divide time into seven-day increments, and any attempts to map Tunica days to the European concept of a week would either be skewed or entirely contrived. Mapping the documented Tunica words for months of the year is even more confounding. It is not entirely clear what calendric system was used by Tunica people in the past. Several area groups, including the Natchez and the Choctaw, used a quasi-lunar thirteen-month calendar (Le Page du Pratz [1763] 1947, 336–43; Swanton 1931, 44). However, the Tunica linguistic record does not clearly lend itself to any known calendar. Both Gatschet/Swanton and Youchigant/Haas recorded a seven-month calendar, but only one name is found in both calendars.

Of the seven month names recorded by Gatschet and Swanton (n.d.) in the late 1880s, six come in pairs: *tahch'awɛka tehukuma* 'February' literally means "January's younger sister"; *komelitahch'a tehukuma* 'April' is literally "March's younger sister"; and *tihikatahch'a tehukuma* 'July' is "June's younger sister." *Tahch'ayruru* 'May' (lit. "long moon") is the only month given by Gatschet and Swanton's informants that does not have a sister counterpart.

Forty years later, Youchigant told Haas that he could not recall any day or month names, though "the old folks knew them" (Haas n.d.a., 8:103). However, as he continued to remember the language, he eventually recalled seven names. Youchigant's Tunica month names, save one, are entirely different from those recorded by Gatschet and Swanton, though several of their English glosses overlap. In general, the Tunica month names that Youchigant provides relate to colors; no reference to the "sister" relationship found in Gatschet and Swanton appears in Youchigant's set of months. May, June, July, and a month with no English gloss translate to "white month," "yellow month," "red month," and "black month," respectively. In addition, Haas documents *tahch'asap'ara* 'cold month' and *tahch'aruwina* 'hot month'. *Tahch'ayuru* is only Tunica term used by both generations of Tunica speakers; Tunica speaker Ely Johnson told Gatschet and Swanton that the English gloss was "May," but Youchigant does not give any equivalent Gregorian month for the word, calling it "unknown month." While these terms are linguistically and culturally fascinating, none of them provide us with a comprehensive picture of pre-contact Tunica calendrics.

Regardless of the calendrics used by the Tunica of yore, contemporary speakers need a cohesive set of Tunica months that maps to the Gregorian calendar. To that end, KYLY created a new set of month names in Tunica. The revitalized system is a mixture of documented forms and neologisms. For example, *tahch'asap'ara* 'cold month' was kept in its documented Tunica form, but it now means December instead of September. *Tahch'ahipu* (lit. "dance moon") is the neologism for May, in recognition of the Tunica-Biloxi Tribe's annual pow-wow.

The *tehukuma* 'her younger sister' pattern documented by Gatschet was maintained and expanded. The term was used for previously documented and new forms alike. For example, *Tahch'aruwina* (lit. "hot moon") was documented by Gatschet and Swanton as August. Many KYLY members felt that August was related to September (perhaps because they are both early fall months, or perhaps due to their similar weather patterns in Louisiana, or possibly because they both encompass a back-to-school feel). Regardless, *Tahch'aruwina Tehukuma* is the neologism created for September, modeled on the sister pattern of older Tunica.

With the month names decided, it was time to figure out what to do with them in the dictionary. To recap, we now have three different sets of recorded Tunica months: Gatschet and Swanton's set from the 1880s, Haas's set from the 1930s, and the contemporary set. Should all forms be included in the New Tunica Dictionary? Should only the newest set be published? Should the Tunica–English side of the dictionary be identical to the English–Tunica side, or should they be different? One strategy in such cases is to keep all forms of the language from all points in time, with labels such as *archaic, obsolete,* or *historical* to alert the dictionary user that certain forms are not actively in use. An obsolete headword may even go so far as to link to the contemporary form of the word, guiding users who hope to produce the language to the correct dictionary entry. There are several strategies; in order to help KYLY decide on a version, I drew up the following examples. Note that there is considerable variation between these entries in order to show a range of possible outputs.

Tunica–English
Tahch'asap'ara: *n.* 1) December 2) *obsolete,* September

Tahch'ayuru: May in contemporary Tunica, or July in old Tunica, *cf.*
Tahch'ahipu, Tihikatahch'a Tehukuma

English–Tunica
May: 1) Tahch'ahipu 2) Tahch'ayuru, *historical* 3) Tahch'arɔwa *obsolete,*
dubious

July: 1) Tihikatahch'a Tehukuma **2)** *obsolete,* Tahch'ayuru **3)** *obsolete,*
Tahch'amili

Each of these options provides a full, comprehensive picture of the Tunica language through time. If Tunica learners encounter a month word in a historical written context, the above entries provide them with enough information to decipher the word's meaning. But these approaches clutter the entries' presentation. When trying to produce new Tunica phrases, which is currently a process of translating from English to Tunica, a user may ignore labels and use the wrong word for the month of July because the older forms are shorter. Or in working from the Tunica–English side of a dictionary, a user may give up trying to find the word for May because there are three separate entries. These are all examples of failures of dictionary design in that the user did not correctly find the word sought.

In all fairness, these issues are not unique to revitalization dictionaries. Major lexicographic publishing houses such as *Merriam-Webster* and the *Oxford English Dictionary* have been forced to grapple with the strain between entries that encourage the production of contemporary language and those needed for the passive reading of older historical texts. An article by Margaret Hartmann (2011), sensationally titled "Oxford English Dictionary Cuts 'Cassette Tape' to Make Room for 'Mankini,'" lambasts lexicographers for removing older words to make room for newer words in the *Concise Oxford English Dictionary*. The dictionary's editors were quick to point out that the term *cassette tape* is not disappearing from their unabridged dictionaries, but that the term is no longer relevant for a small collegiate reference meant for the production of college papers. Once again, the anticipated or expressed needs of the user dictate the inclusion or exclusion of information. Obsolete words are not important to the production of language and are thus frequently culled from abridged dictionaries.[7] However, obsolete words could be encountered in reading older texts, making their inclusion important on the reception side of a bilingual dictionary. By this logic, if a user wants to produce Tunica month names, going from English to Tunica, they only need to know the

7. The unabridged *Oxford English Dictionary* has more than 215,000 words, of which at least 47,000 are considered obsolete. This dictionary is a complete historical record of all English and, when printed, spans more than twenty volumes. Most of the obsolete words are excluded from Oxford Dictionaries' other dictionaries (Oxford Dictionaries 2018).

contemporary forms of the language. If they are working with archival materials, going from Tunica to English, they may need access to older word forms. If they are researching the calendric systems of southeastern peoples, they may want to see a comparison of all month names across time. Ultimately, the selection of information should be driven by how a user will use the dictionary.

In the New Tunica Dictionary, month words have been tagged for surfacing in different kinds of dictionaries for digital filtering. However, print dictionaries do not have this luxury, and the natural division of labor between the Tunica–English and English–Tunica sides of the dictionary have resulted in different information on both sides. For the month of May, final entries in the print dictionary appear like so:

Tunica–English

Tahch'ahipu *cf.* **Tahch'arɔwa, Tahch'ayuru** (**tahch'a, hipu** "Dancing Month") *nprop* May *Tach'ahipu yukatihch, ingachihchi tihkashuhki pataku.* Mother's Day falls during May. *Tayoroniku-Halayihku nih-kirhipu yaku Tach'ahiputɛpan.* The Tunica-Biloxi have their pow-wow every May.

Tahch'arɔwa *cf.* **Tahch'ahipu** (**tahch'a, rɔwa** "white month") *n* May, in old Tunica *Wantaha tahch'ahchi sinkuhta tahch'arɔwa tetisa. Hɛ'ɛsh Tahch'ahipu tetisa.* Long ago the fifth month was called "white month." Now it is called "Dancing Month." {obso}

Tahch'ayuru *cf.* **Tahch'ahipu, Tihikatahch'a Tehukuma** (**tahch'a, yuru** "long month") *n* July or May, in old Tunica *Tahch'ahipu tihkashuhkis-inima yuru pirati. Tihikatahch'a Tehukuma ashuhkisinima yuru. Sesostrie Youchigant hɛtahch'asinima "tahch'ayuru" sinkwaliku.* In May the days get long. In July the days are long. Sesostrie Youchigant called these months "long month." {obso}

English–Tunica

May *nprop* Tahch'ahipu *Tach'ahipu yukatihch, ingachihchi tihkashuhki pataku.* Mother's Day falls during May. *Tayoroniku-Halayihku nih-kirhipu yaku Tach'ahiputɛpan.* The Tunica-Biloxi have their pow-wow every May.

The difference in information on the two sides of the print dictionary is intentional: the Tunica–English side supports receptive language activities by offering ample historical information; the English–Tunica side supports productive language activities by displaying only contemporary Tunica forms.

Using Vocabulary Gaps as Lexicographic Opportunity

Languages of all vitality status have gaps in their lexicon. English does not have two distinct words for "mother's mother" and "father's mother" like Swedish does. Spanish contains no good translation for "awkward." Healthy, vibrant languages fill in lexical gaps when needed through borrowing, coinage, compounding, and other language-specific neologistic strategies. But languages of endangered or revitalizing status often need to be more deliberate in filling those gaps. Tunica's lexicon was frozen in 1948, more than sixty years before the TLP got its start. Not only did the frozen lexicon fail to evolve with the times, it but it recorded a point in Tunica's history when the language was in a state of near disuse. It was not uncommon for the last speaker, Youchigant, to remember a word in Tunica but be unable to recall the translation in English or French. This situation resulted in many Tunica words being dutifully recorded by Haas with "doubtful" glosses.

One area of stark ambiguity and doubt in Youchigant's lexicon pertained to flora and fauna. In Haas's 1953 *Tunica Dictionary*, many words pertaining to plants and animals are simply missing. Many others refer to unidentified plants and animals that Youchigant could not render into either French or English. Haas glosses several different Tunica words with the phrase "bird species," "insect species," or "oak species," among others. The Tunica words themselves are compounds and therefore descriptive. For example, Haas lists five different entries for "vine," only two of which are identified. The others, *yishihɔsani, uwatayahpu,* and *hɔsanrɔwa,* are glossed uniformly as "vine species," but each has a distinct literal definition: "raccoon vine," "owl poisoner," and "white vine," respectively. *Shilatakɔra,* identified as an unknown fern species, literally means "worm drinker." However, these literal translations are entirely meaningless to an English speaker, which makes them of no use in the production of contemporary Tunica. If a dictionary is meant to be used for language production, it must contain distinct entries with unambiguous definitions (Zgusta 1971; Sterkenburg 2003; Svensén 2009).

A large set of unidentified species vocabulary pertained to birds. One method of aligning these words with distinct English words would have been to consult with an ornithologist. This option would have allowed us to not only identify ambiguous bird terminology but create new terminology for birds based on expertise. However, such a practice would have excluded the larger learning community. Words would have appeared in the dictionary as "real" words that a learner would "just memorize." While this top-down approach might have alleviated my needs as a lexicographer, it did not address the learning community's need for context and an understanding of how to construct new words in Tunica.

And so, under the auspices of KYLY, I proposed a bird-theme summer camp in 2016. The theme encompassed several important aspects of Tunica language and culture. Area conservationists and bird-watchers were invited to give talks about local birds, during which events participants volunteered Tunica vocabulary. Tunica stories portraying birds as protagonists were dramatized by campgoers. Traditional regalia and other pow-wow traditions featuring feathers were explained. One highlight of the 2016 Tunica summer camp was a session conducted around bird neologisms. Two identical sessions for neologisms were run, one with older students (ages 12–18), and one with younger students (ages 5–11). The goal of the sessions was twofold: (1) to introduce campers to the process of making new words, something they had not previously been encouraged to do, and (2) to create neologisms for eight birds familiar to the learners but lacking from the dictionary (ostrich, penguin, peacock, swan, pheasant, parrot, toucan, and flamingo).

To start each session, I addressed the entire group of students. I opened with a brief explanation of why these words were not in Tunica already. It makes sense, in the case of penguins and ostriches, that Tunica had no corresponding names; the learners' Tunica ancestors would not have seen these birds, nor would they have interacted with peoples who knew these birds, trading for their feathers or whatnot. But in today's world, one might go to the zoo, see a penguin, and want to talk to their friend about it in Tunica. This opening was imperative for two reasons. First, it acknowledges the gaps in the Tunica language without presenting the language as deficient and therefore illegitimate. Second, it opens the space to discuss how creating new words is a central part of being a Tunica speaker. Neologisms are not outliers in any language; vibrant speaker communities regularly make new words to fill their needs. Tunica is no exception. One need only look at the wide array of neologisms KYLY has created for its work to see that new word creation is fundamental to the revitalization and production of Tunica. As long as neologisms are created with internal Tunica grammatical rules in mind, neologisms are in fact authentic Tunica.

The second activity of the session was to brainstorm, as a large group, features of a bird that one could use in making a neologism. Campers offered a wide range of features that could characterize a given bird: (1) physical features, such as coloration, neck length, and beak size; (2) method of movements, such as whether a bird flies, swims, or runs; (3) habitat, such as whether it lives in cold or hot climates, in swamps or deserts; (4) nest-building practices; (5) food sources; and (6) migration patterns.

Each learner suggestion was validated, and it was explained that a word becomes a word when a person uses it, her friends use it, and they understand each other. From there, the larger group was broken up into smaller groups containing four students. Each group had at least one adult participant who was familiar with the Tunica language. Groups were given a list of the birds, pictures of the fowl, and a bag of Tunica morphemes to use in the creation of new words. The morphemes, printed on individual strips of paper, were cut at different angles to indicate whether they were a root, suffix, or prefix. This practice was meant to guide morpheme order while learners created words. The morphemes were in Tunica only; no English was present on the slip. The exercise challenged students to recall the words they knew, though they could also ask their adult participant about the meanings of certain words. Because the New Tunica Dictionary digital app did not yet exist, groups were also told that they could request a Haas dictionary if they wanted to know words for their neologisms that were not present in their morpheme bag. This practice served to limit the campers' exposure to unfamiliar orthography unless they were excited to learn more. Excitement tends to be great impetus for overcoming unfamiliar challenges. Of the eight groups, only two asked for access to the Haas dictionary. Students would give suggestions for bird names, and adult participants helped direct them in a grammatically valid construction of that word.

The creativity of campers filled the room, as learners debated the core characteristics of various fowl and ways to render the terminology in Tunica. A sampling of student proposals is as follows:

rihkukuwahtoku mili 'flamingo'—lit. "red stick bird"

takuwatohku hilaku milisha 'flamingo'—lit. "pink bird who is shaky"

kaliɔshkasahku 'flamingo'—lit. "one leg standing"

kuwatohku tewali halisɔpani 'ostrich'—lit. "fast bird of the wild lands"

talɔt'osinilupi 'ostrich'—lit. "bald-headed runner"

takuwatohku yanahta panu 'parrot'—lit. "very chatty bird"

ushtanakosu 'toucan'—lit. "colorful beak"

takuwatohku tawihu kosu risa 'peacock'—lit. "spotted fan bird of many colors"

ushtosulɔta 'peacock'—lit. "running eye"

One of my favorite comments was a question as to whether morphemes from the bag could be used in more than one bird name. The morpheme in question was *rukaya* 'dangerous'. The group wanted to name peacock *rukayakuwatohku* (lit. "danger bird") because the spots on a peacock's tail look like eyes, and any animal who sees it would think "danger." The other bird that the group felt should be labeled *rukaya* was the ostrich.

Students of all ages had fun with and found value in this exercise. Older students had heated discussions about the validity of certain characteristics in a neologism; one learner was insistent that peacocks were very protective, and that a word for peacock that did not incorporate this aspect was not valid. Younger learners enjoyed putting morphemes together in random order and then eagerly asking "what does this mean??" As I walked the room, I received one such inquiry, in which the students had combined *mili* and *tɛwali*, literally meaning "fast red." I told the students the literal translation and asked what kind of bird they thought could be described as "fast red." They excitedly yelled out suggestions, including "hummingbird!" "parrot!" and "dragon!" The last option garnered the most support from the group.

The success of the exercise was immediately apparent, as noted by both staff and students. The successes included the following:

- Students were encouraged to think metaphorically about the Tunica language. A popular translation for flamingo was *rihkumili* or "red stick." Two groups incorporated the eye-like spots on a peacock's tail into their word for peacock.
- Learners gained a more thorough understanding of Tunica morphology.
  - Though words such as morpheme, affixation, clitic, and root were never used in the sessions, student were exposed to the morphological rules involved in compounding.
  - Students took this new understanding to their learning outside of the session. For example, one teenage camper stopped in front of the craft table (a table that he had walked by each of the previous three days) and said, "hey wait! *Kosuwishi*, the word for paint. That just means 'colored water'?!"
- The sessions instilled excitement and a sense of ownership in the language. Students were eager to see *their* word in the New Tunica Dictionary.

The neologism workshop has become a recurring event of the annual immersion sessions and summer camps. New words for weather, constellations, careers, and bugs have been created in this setting. But more than meeting a linguistic need, these workshops have leveraged the dictionary for a shift in the attitude toward the Tunica language. Gaps in the lexicon are no longer seen as deficiencies; they are opportunities. Tunica learners see gaps in the language as chances to get their word into the dictionary, a feat that imparts the inherent prestige of the dictionary to the word's creator. Exercises such as these are imperative for the continued expansion of the Tunica language. Using the dictionary to foster linguistic creativity in an interactive setting encourages students to explore what their language could be within the grammatical confines inherent in Tunica.

Conclusion

Neologisms pose specific challenges for all lexicographers. When to include them, how to include them, and where to include them are all questions that lexicographers must answer when dealing with neologisms. However, these same words also provide a unique opportunity. The creativity and linguistic investment of speakers in creating new words is a powerful resource, essential for successful language revitalization efforts. The New Tunica Dictionary sought to minimize the stigmatization of new words and decided to include them on equal standing with older Tunica word forms. In some cases, the New Tunica Dictionary even prefers neologisms to older forms, as we saw with Tunica month names. Activities undertaken with language learners over the course of the dictionary's compilation have sought to encourage learners to be bold in their expansion of Tunica's domains through the creation of new words; integrating these words into the new dictionary legitimizes the learners' efforts and encourages further creativity. Notably, some Tunica speakers now see neologism creation as an essential component of their dictionary. Lintinger's quote at the beginning of the chapter ends with "of course"; of course, the dictionary has sparked conversations of new words and concepts in Tunica. Tunica speakers are eager to see their new words in the dictionary; and new words are being created on a regular basis. Moving forward, it is imperative that a mechanism for moving neologisms from these sessions into the dictionary be established. The quick adaptation of neologisms into the dictionary ensures that the New Tunica Dictionary remains a useful and supportive resource for Tunica speakers.

Chapter Six
New Tunica Dictionary at Large

The New Tunica Dictionary has altered the way in which present-day Tunica speakers interact with the language. Speakers now have a quick reference to contemporary Tunica forms.

> Having the dictionary at my fingertips whenever I need it makes it much easier to find words on the fly. It can be really exciting to discover new words and incorporate them into conversation. If I need to translate something on the fly, I can whip out my phone and have an answer in seconds.
>
> Tyler Whitaker, Tunica Language Project (TLP) linguist

Teachers report using the dictionary in their classrooms; speakers use it in their homes.

> *Webonary asuhkitɛpan ashuyuru pahita wali kichu ihkara. Kata? Ritetimili kichu, hɔwashi hotu, ihkri kichu, katotu.*
>
> I use Webonary every day on my phone. Where? In the classroom, also outside of it, in my house, everywhere.
>
> Ya Nuhchi, Donna Pierite, master language teacher[1]

---

1. Author's translation.

Getting the dictionary into the hands of speakers is an ongoing project, one that has taken more time than anticipated during the dictionary's initial planning. Tunica speakers currently have access to the dictionary in two digital formats, and a print version of the dictionary is under construction as of 2020. The unanticipated hurdles encountered in distributing the New Tunica Dictionary merit discussion; despite the difficulties, there are options for small lexicographic projects to get their product into community hands.

Tunica Dictionary Distribution

The TLP always intended for the dictionary to appear in both print and digital versions. To date, the Tunica dictionary team works with three different dictionary outputs, all based on the same FLEx data: a phone app, a website, and a print dictionary. The dictionary project has benefited greatly from the understanding that the dictionary would be published in several forms and that each would be released on its own timeline. This approach has allowed the Tunica working group (Kuhpani Yoyani Luhchi Yoroni, KYLY) to distribute the dictionary in different media with different forms of "readiness," which has sped up access to the dictionary by learners.

KYLY decided that the digital dictionary would be available first; the digital format was desirable given the comparatively low cost of distribution and ease of updates. We could pilot versions and easily change the dictionary based on user feedback. KYLY has several other ongoing projects to increase the online presence of Tunica, lest it be judged as antiquated or unable to keep up with modernity; a digital dictionary fit into the overall objective of presenting Tunica as a modern language. KYLY recognized that a print dictionary would be a large investment; however, from the beginning, a print dictionary was considered to be an important end product. Print dictionaries carry much weight, sometimes quite literally, and it is difficult to replicate the pride and satisfaction of holding a tangible dictionary in one's hands. The paths to publishing and distributing these various media have continuously evolved over the New Tunica Dictionary's lifetime.

Tunica Dictionary App

When the New Tunica Dictionary was first proposed in 2013, the digital dictionary was intended to be an online resource, such as a website. However, technologies have changed drastically in the last eight years; the success of the smartphone and the use of phone apps have altered the technological landscape in unforeseen ways. Apps are now the easiest way to have information at one's fingertips, an impressive development given that the Google Play store did not even launch until March 2012, two years after the TLP was initiated. Dictionaries have not been left behind in this digital revolution, and many Indigenous and Native American language apps are available through both Google Play and the iTunes app store. Given their popularity, I began exploring ways to deliver a Tunica dictionary app in lieu of a dictionary website.

On March 7, 2016, SIL International developers released a program called the Dictionary App Builder, which enables those using FLEx to quickly make a dictionary app for mobile devices (SIL 2020). This software takes FLEx-exported XML documents and, with a properly configured development environment and the click of a button, produces a ready-made dictionary app for Android devices. The ease of this software is extraordinary; the initial setup took a few hours, but subsequent updates to the app take a matter of minutes. The high degree of user friendliness makes the Dictionary App Builder very appealing; this software can be used by any tribally appointed staff member regardless of technological expertise.

However, there are several drawbacks to the app builder. Because the app building process is automated, certain formatting decisions are not allowed. For example, I can customize the app with font and background colors, but I cannot specify the order of alphabetization, which is problematic for letters such as ɛ, ɔ, and glottal stop (ɛ and ɔ appear at the end of the alphabetized list, while glottal stop appears at the beginning). Another limitation is that the software is centered on creating Android apps. As of January 2019, when we most recently attempted to tackle an iOS app, the App Builder iOS apps had limited features and did not allow users to search the dictionary.[2] However, the most annoying shortcoming of apps generated through the Dictionary App Builder is that compound Tunica

2. Expanding the functionality of iOS apps is a high priority for the SIL Dictionary App Builder team, and its features will likely be greatly improved at the time of this book's publication (SIL, pers. comm.).

words on the Tunica–English list (when accessed via browse, not search) do not appear as their own headwords. Rather, they appear under their constituent morphemes. A user scrolling through the app in search of *hahpu* 'to shower' would not find it as a headword but would need to look under *ha-* or *ahpu* (in contrast to the English–Tunica side, where *shower* appears as its own headword). While this issue is highly problematic in theory, I have found that, in reality, most users look for words via search (which returns headword-like entries for *hahpu*) rather than by manually scrolling through the letters, so the issue does not seem to affect overall usability of the app.

Despite its shortcomings, the benefits of the Dictionary App Builder are substantial. Example sentences and audio files are automatically populated on their entries. One can search alphabetically or by keyword in either English or Tunica. All these features are baked into the software; there is no need to write computer code. The app can be easily updated simply by re-exporting the latest FLEx data and running the Dictionary App Builder software. The app is used regularly by members of KYLY, and it was first piloted by language learners at the youth immersion workshop in January 2017. Reports from users have been positive.

The dictionary is indispensable to the work we do. It makes it so easy to quickly translate something, come up with games, lesson ideas, visual aids, social media, etc. Pretty much wherever we are we can direct someone to the dictionary to find a word. At our recent summer camp, our brand-new volunteer teachers with only a week of Tunica experience were able to lead groups of students in neologism creation using only the dictionary app.

Tyler Whitaker, TLP linguist

Given the success of the initial launch of the dictionary app, the Tunica-Biloxi Tribe began exploring ways in which the app could be more widely distributed, including publishing it in the Google Play store. The Language and Culture Revitalization Program (LCRP) created a Google Play account, and staff at the LCRP attempted to submit the app for review themselves. However, the Google Play dashboard is designed for developers and technical project managers who are familiar with app development, and staff had several questions about the information that Google Play was asking of them. Fortunately, I am very familiar with such interfaces, given my employment as a software engineer; I worked with the LCRP to gather the necessary details for app submission, such as app screenshots and user ratings.[3] A beta version of the app was submitted to Google Play in May 2019, but it crashed on Pixel 2 phones and so the submission was rejected. Once again, I was grateful we chose a technology solution with an active support team; SIL's Dictionary App Builder team was responsive in working through the issue, and it released a new version of the Dictionary App Builder that fixed the problem. In September 2019, the first version of the New Tunica Dictionary app was released in the Google Play store. Two subsequent updates of the app have been released, in response to new words created during a summer camp and immersion workshop, respectively. Master language teacher Elisabeth Mora suggested that the LCRP track download metrics to see how the community interacts with the dictionary app, noting how it corresponds with LCRP programming. Now that the app is live, we have seen steady trends toward greater download frequency.

Digital Distribution via the Web

The TLP knew from an early stage in distribution planning that a website version of the dictionary would be needed, even after the phone app was identified as a more desirable digital format. Webonary was discovered by a KYLY member as advertised on SIL's website. Again, enticed by the plug-and-play functionality of FLEx data, we built the Webonary version using exported FLEx XML data. The online dictionary is in draft form, with specific "in-progress" aspects of entries' microstructure deliberately hidden at present. The New Tunica Dictionary is online and can be accessed through any web browser from any phone or computer.

The Webonary version of the dictionary was initially created as a stopgap measure, one to temporarily give dictionary access to iOS users while a phone app was under development. However, Webonary use now far outstrips Android app use, and learners are familiar with the format. Students are encouraged to pin the website to their phones' homepage, and Elisabeth Mora has created videos explaining how to effectively use the Webonary site. "One tribal community member who resides in Texas has shared Webonary in a tribal Facebook group. She encouraged others interested in learning to go to the website. This created a ripple effect

---

3. SIL has since improved its documentation of the Dictionary App Builder to include information about the Google Play submission process (SIL 2016).

and resulted in translation requests from at least two other families" (E. Mora, pers. comm.). Translation requests generally arise when dictionary users can't find what they were looking for; a memorable example was a query about how to translate *life*, as in "Water is Life," since this term did not exist in the dictionary. Such phrases are translated by Tunica master teachers and result in Tunica appearing on signs, T-shirts, banners, and fliers within the community. Councilwoman Brenda Lintinger uses the website "whenever I want to express something that I'm not sure of and to remind myself of words I don't use often. The dictionary has become a more valuable tool in day-to-day learning" (pers. comm.). Given this version's renown, it is unlikely to be discontinued even if a usable iOS phone app is developed.

The revitalization project has benefited from having two separately maintained dictionary media. The phone app was initially restricted for download from the TLP shared cloud space; a potential user needed an invite from the group to download the app. Phone app circulation was deliberately restricted; in contrast, the Webonary is a publicly available website locatable through any online search engine (Tunica-Biloxi Tribe 2020).[4] Given the different levels of public visibility, the Tunica working group used the Android app to pilot information and formatting that was not yet fully vetted for public consumption. One example of this practice is in the treatment of example sentences; the Webonary version does not contain any example sentences, while the phone app contains KYLY-vetted examples as entered in FLEx. Now that the Android app is going public, steps are being taken to align the information in these two media more closely. To accomplish this, I created several small programming scripts (in Python) that standardize and scrub the FLEx XML data before it is uploaded to either Webonary or the Dictionary App Builder.

In addition to being popular among Tunica speakers, the Webonary version of the dictionary has features that the phone app does not, such as a comments feature.

---

4. As stated in chapter 1, the Tunica-Biloxi Tribe is not opposed to its language being shared with noncommunity members. Instead, tribal members take pride in sharing their language and the strides they have made to reclaim it, which makes a publicly available site like Webonary ideal for hosting the Tunica dictionary. In communities in which restricting access is a priority, a website owned by the community can better serve this need, as it can be restricted to approved users or networked computers.

> I would like to see more activity in the "comments" feature of Webonary, specifically for user-generated examples or questions (e.g., "Can I use this word this way?" "Does this sentence make sense?" etc.). We can use this data to gauge where the most interest is and what the most common questions are.
>
> Tyler Whitaker, TLP linguist

Future phases of the digital dictionary include implementing ways in which Tunica speakers can easily submit neologisms to a dictionary editorial board for review and inclusion in the dictionary. As with the Dictionary App Builder, limitations to the Webonary platform are general customizability; because SIL hosts the dictionary, we cannot rearrange the layout or adjust the font. We cannot add features like a custom "word of the day" widget, something easily done if we had full control via our own website. However, the available features are meeting current user needs. Moreover, SIL hosts the site, pays for its maintenance, and is available for questions or troubleshooting. SIL (2015) clearly states that the uploaders maintain all intellectual property rights of their content. In short, the trade-offs of using Webonary are acceptable to Tunica leadership, and the response from Tunica speakers to the platform indicates that Webonary will be officially supported by the TLP for the foreseeable future.

Print Dictionary

The finality of a printed dictionary is both satisfying and daunting. Members of the TLP sense the gravity of a print dictionary and very much want one; however, there is also recognition that, once printed, the dictionary is unlikely to be updated for many years due to the prohibitive typesetting and printing costs. Therefore, both KYLY and the LCRP express a strong desire for the dictionary to be "final" before printing.

> Some community members may prefer a physical copy of the dictionary.... A published physical copy could be made available through the [Tunica-Biloxi Cultural and Educational Resources Center] gift shop, however I think we should address the most pressing issues before pursuing dictionary publication.
>
> Elisabeth Mora, master language teacher

After the first neologism workshop in 2016, Tunica community members expressed a desire to take over the final stages of data entry and editing of the New Tunica Dictionary. I was incredibly honored and humbled by this consensus. When I started work on the dictionary three years prior, my goal was not merely to make a dictionary, but to make a *community* dictionary, one in which the Tunica-speaking community is vested. The groundswell of interest and commitment on the part of tribal community members indicated my goal had been realized. The LCRP has already taken steps to move aspects of the lexicographic process into the hands of Tunica speakers. For example, the Tunica-Biloxi Tribe now hosts annual immersion sessions for Tunica learners, in which youth are trained in language teaching, with a focus on the process of making neologisms. Steps have been taken to attain equipment and train community members in audio recording in preparation for recording sound clips for dictionary entries. The LCRP has identified several tasks to be completed before the final production of a published print dictionary, including: (1) a full, community-backed editorial pass on the FLEx database, ensuring that all fields are filled out in a uniform manner; (2) the addition of example sentences for every subsense of all headwords; and (3) approval of the final version of the dictionary by tribal leadership. As of the writing of this book, the print version of the New Tunica Dictionary is still progressing through its editorial phases, with no clear timeline as to when it will be ready for publication. KYLY intends to submit the dictionary for print once all example sentences have been approved and content has been fully vetted by the Tribe's leadership.

Once the dictionary is finalized, the Tunica-Biloxi Tribe will secure a means of publication. The Tribe has completed several Tribe-sponsored publications, such as a new edition of the 1987 book *The Tunica-Biloxi Tribe, Its Culture and People* (Klopotek 2017). There is a preference for self-publication, as it allows the copyright and intellectual property to remain firmly with the Tunica-Biloxi. However, given the complexity of dictionary formatting, it is possible that the dictionary will be published with an established press. If this is the case, Tunica-Biloxi leadership will review any publishing contract to ensure that the Tribe retains copyright and intellectual property.[5]

---

5. Issues concerning copyright and intellectual property rights of languages have been documented by several Native American groups, including the Koasati (Langley et al. 2018) and the Hopi (Hill 2002).

The Future of the New Tunica Dictionary

Since the dictionary's distribution, I have noticed increased active participation from students in immersion breakout sessions, during which no written Tunica materials or English language is allowed. Immediately upon completion of the session, speakers whip out their digital dictionaries to double check a construction they tried out or to explain a phrase they kept repeating but that no one understood. This is, of course, a correlative observation; speakers undoubtably become more active due to their increased familiarity with the language over time. But the consistent reference to the dictionary after these sessions prompts me to wonder about its role in encouraging speakers to take risks and make mistakes while speaking; the assurances that a dictionary is nearby to help correct or facilitate communication seems to embolden Tunica speakers. This linguistic risk-taking is an important step in developing proficient, communicative speakers. Even when the dictionary is used in the "I was right, you were wrong" sense, a use I do not advocate, this activity does not appear to shut down language production among Tunica learners. Instead, easy access to this lexicographic knowledge and authority seems to embolden speakers to try out new constructions.

> I reference Webonary to make sure I'm saying the right word in Tunica and also to look up words I do not know the Tunica word for.
>
> Teyanna Pierite-Simon, Tunica language apprentice

I would venture that mere existence of the Tunica dictionary, the fact that there is a right and a wrong, has shifted perspective on Tunica language production by community members from a fear that they are just making things up, to a pride in their ability to speak verifiable Tunica.

Tunica language presence in online spaces has increased since the dictionary was made available. Multiple KYLY members stated that they regularly consult the dictionary when posting online. While Tunica language could be found online prior to the dictionary, most uses were single words or short phrases. KYLY member Brett Nelson reports that the dictionary "allows me to create more and more complex sentences for use in social media." I am encouraged by the explosion of Tunica language use and the ongoing efforts of the overall revitalization project, which help ensure that linguistic creativity and community-driven effort will continue to be funneled into the New Tunica Dictionary. In fact, dictionary users have already suggested several improvements they would like to implement in future iterations of the dictionary.

> I would like to include audio or video pronunciation and images where appropriate in Webonary, especially for entries that contain information culturally significant to the Tribe or Avoyelles Parish.
>
> Elisabeth Mora, master language teacher

> Where would I like to see the dictionary go? In two years: published with all the example sentences. In five years, with more cultural content sentences from Gatschet and perhaps from some of the Sesostrie texts. In 20 years, with lots of neologisms and new slang, contemporary uses updating the historical texts. I'd like to see coinages from new speakers that occur spontaneously and are documented, as well as the neologisms from the structured exercises of the summer camps.
>
> Judith M. Maxwell, Louise Rebecca Schawe and
> Williedell Schawe Professor of Linguistics and Anthropology

Desires for improvements notwithstanding, the New Tunica Dictionary is already considered by community members to be an anchor of the language revitalization project.

> Certainly, I believe [the dictionary] should and will continue to expand as new discoveries and achievements in society arise and evolve. I feel excited to know that we are building this collection of information in such a way as to avoid any loss in the future, especially in light of how close we came to losing the Tunica language. . . . [The group's] work may very well enable the Tunica language to live in perpetuity. That is a profound accomplishment!
>
> Brenda Lintinger, Tunica-Biloxi councilwoman

In my ongoing work with the New Tunica Dictionary, I continue to encourage speakers to reimagine the dictionary as more than just perfunctory reference material. Decoupling dictionaries from the common perception that they are unbiased, scientific objects does not, in my opinion, devalue their contributions to revitalization. Quite the contrary: reimagining dictionaries as deeply narrative works highlights the points of entry for speech community input and elevates their long-term usability. Such community-driven texts then move on to serve a wide range of functions in the larger revitalization effort, celebrating the passion and dedication of the community to the preservation and advancement of its language.

Hɛrowina hot'ɔp'uhki. Teti hotut'ɛhɛshkan. Hishtahahki Luhchi Yoroni wichiku.

Bibliography

Al-Ajmi, Hashan. 2002. "Which Microstructural Features of Bilingual Dictionaries Affect Users' Look-Up Performance?" *International Journal of Lexicography* 15 (2): 119–31.

Anderson, Patricia. 2016. "Translaryngeal Phonological Processes in Tunica: An Optimality Theory Approach." *Fleur-De-Ling: Tulane University Working Papers in Linguistics* 2:23–38.

Anderson, Patricia. 2017. "Yanatame Nisa Luhchi Yoroni: Lexicography, Language Revitalization, and the New Tunica Dictionary." PhD diss., Tulane University.

Anderson, Patricia, and Judith M. Maxwell. 2019. "The Tunica Language." In *Language in Louisiana: Community and Culture*, edited by Nathalie Dajko and Shana Walton, 45–63. Jackson: University Press of Mississippi.

Anderson, Patricia, and Judith M. Maxwell. Forthcoming. "Tunica." In *The Languages and Linguistics of Indigenous North America*, vol. 1, edited by Carmen Jany, Marianne Mithun, and Keren Rice. Boston: De Gruyter Mouton.

Aoki, Haruo. 1994. *Nez Perce Dictionary*. Berkeley: University of California Press.

Atkins, Sue B. T. 1996. "Bilingual Dictionaries: Past, Present and Future." In *Proceedings of the 7th EURALEX International Congress*, edited by Martin Gellerstam, Jerker Järborg, Sven Göran Malmgren, Kerstin Norén, Lena Rogström, and Catalina Röjder Papmehl, 515–46. Göteborg, Sweden: Novum Grafiska AB.

Ball, Jessica, and Pauline Janyst. 2008. "Enacting Research Ethics in Partnerships with Indigenous Communities in Canada: 'Do It in a Good Way.'" *Journal of Empirical Research on Human Research Ethics* 3 (2): 33–51.

Baret, John. 1574. *An Alvearie or Triple Dictionarie in Englishe, Latin and French*. Shakespeare's Beehive. Last updated April 18, 2018. https://shakespearesbeehive.com.

Bartholomew, Doris A., and Louise C. Schoenhals. 1983. "Special Grammatical Designations for Indigenous Languages." In *Bilingual Dictionaries for Indigenous Languages*, 161–77. Mexico: Summer Institute of Linguistics.

Batz, Alexandre de. 1732. *Buffalo Tamer, Chief of the Tunica*. Smithsonian Misc. Collections, vol. 80, no. 5, plate 2. National Anthropological Archives, Smithsonian Institution, Washington, D.C.

Benedicto, Elena. 2018. "When Participatory Action Research (PAR) and (Western) Academic Institutional Policies Do Not Align." In Bischoff and Jany 2018, 38–65.

Bergenholtz, Henning. 2011. "Access to and Presentation of Needs-Adapted Data in Monofunctional Internet Dictionaries." In Fuertes-Olivera and Bergenholtz 2011, 30–53.

Bergenholtz, Henning, Theo Bothma, and Rufus H. Gouws. 2011. "A Model for Integrated Dictionaries of Fixed Expressions." In *Electronic Lexicography in the 21st Century: New Applications for New Users: Proceedings of eLex 2011*, edited by Iztok Kosem and Karmen Kosem, 34–42. Bled, Slovenia: Trojína, Institute for Applied Slovene Studies.

Bergenholtz, Henning, and Rufus H. Gouws. 2012. "What Is Lexicography?" *Lexikos* 22:31–42.

Bergenholtz, Henning, and Sven Tarp. 2003. "Two Opposing Theories: On H.E. Wiegand's Recent Discovery of Lexicographic Functions." *HERMES: Journal of Language and Communication in Business* 16 (31): 171–96.

Bischoff, Shannon T., and Carmen Jany, eds. 2018. *Insights from Practices in Community-Based Research*. Berlin: De Gruyter.

Bothma, Theo J. D. 2011. "Filtering and Adapting Data and Information in an Online Environment in Response to User Needs." In Fuertes-Olivera and Bergenholtz 2011, 71–102.

Boyer, Ernest L. 1990. *Scholarship Reconsidered: Priorities of the Professoriate*. Princeton, N.J.: Princeton University Press.

Brain, Jeffrey P. 1977. *On the Tunica Trail*. Archaeological Report no. 1. Submitted to Office of State Parks, Department of Culture, Recreation and Tourism. Baton Rouge: Louisiana Archaeological Survey and Antiquities Commission.

Brain, Jeffrey P. 1988. *Tunica Archaeology*. Papers of the Peabody Museum, vol. 78. Cambridge, Mass.: Harvard University Press.

Brain, Jeffrey P. 1990. *The Tunica-Biloxi*. New York: Chelsea House.

Bringle, Robert G., and Julie A. Hatcher. 2002. "Campus-Community Partnerships: The Terms of Engagement." *Journal of Social Issues* 48 (3): 503–16.

Brown, Ian W. 1981. *The Role of Salt in Eastern North American Prehistory*. Baton Rouge: Louisiana, Archeological Survey and Antiquities Commission.

Cablitz, Gabriele H. 2011. "Documenting Cultural Knowledge in Dictionaries of Endangered Languages." In Ogilvie 2011a, 446–62.

Carr, Michael. 1997. "Internet Dictionaries and Lexicography." *International Journal of Lexicography* 10 (3): 209–30.

Cawdrey, Robert. 1604. *A Table Alphabeticall of Hard Usual English Words*. Edited by Raymond G. Siemens. Last updated December 5, 1994. https://onesearch.library.utoronto.ca/sites/default/files/ret/cawdrey/cawdrey0.html.

Chelliah, Shobana. 2001. "The Role of Text Collection and Elicitation in Linguistic Fieldwork." In Newman and Ratliff 2001, 152–65.

Chinuk Wawa Dictionary Project. 2012. *Chinuk Wawa: kakwa nsayka ulman-tilixam laska munk-kemteks nsayka*. Seattle, Wash.: Confederated Tribes of the Grand Ronde Community of Oregon.

Clayton, Mary L., and R. Joe Campbell. 2002. "Alonso de Molina as Lexicographer." In Frawley, Hill, and Munro 2002, 336–90.

COBUILD (Collins Birmingham University International Language Database). n.d. "The History of COBUILD." Accessed February 22, 2019. https://collins.co.uk/pages/elt-cobuild-reference-the-history-of-cobuild.

CODOFIL (Council for the Development of French in Louisiana). 2017. *Annual Report*. https://www.crt.state.la.us/Assets/OCD/codofil/reports/Codofil_annual-report_2016.pdf.

Cohn, Bernard. 1996. *Colonialism and Its Forms of Knowledge: The British in India*. Princeton, NJ: Princeton University Press.

Collins. 2019. "Latest New Word Suggestions." https://www.collinsdictionary.com/us/submissions/latest.

Crowley, Terry. 2007. *Field Linguistics: A Beginner's Guide*. Oxford: Oxford University Press.

Crystal, David. 2000. *Language Death*. Cambridge: Cambridge University Press.

Czaykowska-Higgins, Ewa. 2009. "Research Models, Community Engagement, and Linguistic Fieldwork: Reflections on Working within Canadian Indigenous Communities." *Language Documentation and Conservation* 3 (1): 15–50.

Davis, Jenny L. 2017. "Resisting Rhetorics of Language Endangerment: Reclamation through Indigenous Language Survivance." *Language Documentation and Description* 14:37–58.

Davis, Jenny L. 2018. *Talking Indian: Identity and Language Revitalization in the Chickasaw Renaissance*. Tucson: University of Arizona Press.

Debenport, Erin. 2015. *Fixing the Books: Secrecy, Literacy, and Perfectibility in Indigenous New Mexico*. Santa Fe, N.Mex.: School for Advanced Research Press.

Denzer-King, Ryan. 2008. "Neologisms in Indigenous Languages of North America." *Santa Barbara Papers in Linguistics* 19:25–39.

Dietrich, Wolf. 2015. "The Lexicography of Indigenous Languages in South America." In *International Handbook of Modern Lexis and Lexicography*, edited by Patrick Hanks and Gilles-Maurice de Schryver. Berlin: Springer. http://link-springer-com-443.webvpn.fjmu.edu.cn/referenceworkentry/10.1007/978-3-642-45369-4_91-1.

Doak, Ivy, and Timothy Montler. 2000. "Orthography, Lexicography, and Language Change." In *Endangered Languages and Literacy: Proceedings of the Fourth FEL Conference,* edited by Nicholas Ostler and Blair Rudes, 32–138. Bath: Foundation for Endangered Languages.

Downs, Ernest C. 1979. "The Struggle of the Louisiana Tunica Indians for Recognition." In *Southeastern Indians since the Removal Era*, edited by Walter L. Williams, 72–89. Athens: University of Georgia Press.

Drysdale, P. D. 1987. "The Role of Examples in a Learner's Dictionary." In *The Dictionary and the Language Learner: Papers from the EURALEX Seminar at the University of Leeds, 1–3 April 1985*, edited by Anthony P. Cowie, 213–23. Tübingen, Germany: Niemeyer.

Dziemianko, Anna. 2010. "Paper or Electronic? The Role of Dictionary Form in Language Reception, Production and the Retention of Meaning and Collocations." *International Journal of Lexicography* 23 (3): 257–73.

Eby, John W. 1998. "Why Service-Learning Is Bad." Accessed October 7, 2019. https://www1.villanova.edu/content/dam/villanova/artsci/servicelearning/WhyServiceLearningIsBad.pdf.

Evans, Nicholas. 2001. "The Last Speaker Is Dead—Long Live the Last Speaker!" In Newman and Ratliff 2001, 250–81.

Fabian, Johannes. 1986. *Language and Colonial Power: The Appropriation of Swahili in the Former Belgian Congo, 1880–1938*. Cambridge: Cambridge University Press.

Farrow, Craig. 2019. *FLExTools*. GitHub. Last modified August 21, 2019. https://github.com/cdfarrow/FLExTools/wiki.

Field, Margaret C. 2009. "Metaphor, Mythology, and a Navajo Verb: The Role of Cultural Constructs in the Lexicography of Endangered Languages." *Anthropological Linguistics* 51 (3–4): 296–302. https://doi.org/10.1353/anl.2009.0008.

Frankenberg-Garcia, Ana. 2005. "A Peek into What Today's Language Learners as Researchers Actually Do." *International Journal of Lexicography* 18 (3): 335–55.

Frawley, William J., Kenneth C. Hill, and Pamela Munro, eds. 2002. *Making Dictionaries: Preserving Indigenous Languages of the Americas*. Berkeley: University of California Press.

Fuertes-Olivera, Pedro A., and Henning Bergenholtz, eds. 2011. *e-Lexicography: The Internet, Digital Initiatives and Lexicography*. London: Continuum.

Fuertes-Olivera, Pedro A., and Sven Tarp. 2011. "Lexicography for the Third Millennium: Cognitive-Oriented Specialised Dictionaries for Learners." *Ibérica* 21:141–61.

Gallatin, Albert. 1836. *A Synopsis of the Indian Tribes of North America*. Transactions and Collections of the American Antiquarian Society, vol. 2. Cambridge, Mass.: American Antiquarian Society.

Garrett, Andrew. 2011. "An Online Dictionary with Texts and Pedagogical Tools: The Yurok Language Project at Berkeley." In Ogilvie 2011a, 405–19.

Gatschet, Albert S. 1886a. "Comparative Vocabulary." Manuscript 1011, Albert Samuel Gatschet Papers, 1828–1906. National Anthropological Archives, Smithsonian Institution, Washington, D.C.

Gatschet, Albert S. 1886b. "Letter to the Director of the Bureau of Ethnology, October 24, 1886." Manuscript 1347, Albert Samuel Gatschet Papers, 1828–1906. National Anthropological Archives, Smithsonian Institution, Washington, D.C.

Gatschet, Albert S. 1889. "Sex-Denoting Nouns in American Languages." *Transactions of the American Philological Association* 20:159–71.

Gatschet, Albert S., and John R. Swanton. n.d. Gatschet-Swanton Vocabulary Cards. National Anthropological Archives, Smithsonian Institution, Washington, D.C.

Genee, Inge, and Marie-Odile Junker. 2018. "The Blackfoot Language Resources and Digital Dictionary Project: Creating Integrated Web Resources for Language Documentation and Revitalization." *Language Documentation and Conversation* 12:274–314.

Gouws, Rufus H. 2011. "Learning, Unlearning and Innovation in the Planning of Electronic Dictionaries." In Fuertes-Olivera and Bergenholtz 2011, 17–29.

Gove, Phillip, ed. 1961. *Webster's Third New International Dictionary of the English Language.* New York: Merriam-Webster.

Green, Jonathon. 1996. *Chasing the Sun: Dictionary-Makers and the Dictionaries They Made.* London: Henry Holt.

Grenoble, Lenore A., and Lindsay J. Whaley. 2006. *Saving Languages: An Introduction to Language Revitalization.* Cambridge: Cambridge University Press.

Haas, Mary R. 1940. "Tunica." In *Handbook of American Indian Languages,* vol. 4, edited by Franz Boaz, 1–143. New York: J. J. Augustin.

Haas, Mary R. 1946a. "French Loan-Words in Tunica." *Romance Philology* 1:145–48.

Haas, Mary R. 1946b. "A Grammatical Sketch of Tunica." In *Linguistic Structures of Native America,* edited by Harry Hoijer, 337–66. New York: Viking Fund.

Haas, Mary R. 1950. *Tunica Texts.* University of California Publications in Linguistics, vol. 6, no. 1. Berkeley: University of California Press.

Haas, Mary R. 1951. "The Proto-Gulf Word for 'Water.'" *International Journal of American Linguistics* 17 (2): 71–79.

Haas, Mary R. 1952. "The Proto-Gulf Word for 'Land.'" *International Journal of American Linguistics* 18 (4): 238–41.

Haas, Mary R. 1953. *Tunica Dictionary.* University of California Publications in Linguistics, vol. 6, no. 2. Berkeley: University of California Press.

Haas, Mary R. n.d.a. "Tunica Field Notebooks." Mary Rosamond Haas Papers, Mss. Ms.Coll.94, box 18–20. American Philosophical Society Library, Philadelphia, Pa.

Haas, Mary R. n.d.b. "Unpublished Tunica Grammar." Mary Rosamond Haas Papers, Mss. Ms.Coll.94, box 21. American Philosophical Society Library, Philadelphia, Pa.

Hartmann, Margaret. 2011. "Oxford English Dictionary Cuts 'Cassette Tape' to Make Room for 'Mankini.'" Jezebel.com, October 6, 2011. https://jezebel.com/oxford-english -dictionary-cuts-cassette-tape-to-make-ro-5847061.

Hatton, John. 2011. "Software for Remote Dictionary Collaboration." In Ogilvie 2011a, 420–31.

Heaton, Raina. 2016. "Active-Stative Agreement in Tunica." *Anthropological Linguistics* 58 (3): 299–326.

Heaton, Raina, and Patricia Anderson. 2017. "When Animals Become Humans: Grammatical Gender in Tunica." *International Journal of American Linguistics* 83 (2): 341–63.

Hill, Kenneth C. 2002. "On Publishing the Hopi Dictionary." In Frawley, Hill, and Munro 2002, 299–311.

Hüllen, Werner. 1999. *English Dictionaries, 800–1700: The Topical Tradition.* Oxford: Oxford University Press.

Jeter, Marvin D. 2002. "From Prehistory through Protohistory to Ethnohistory in and near the Northern Lower Mississippi Valley." In *The Transformation of the Southeastern Indians, 1540–1760*, edited by Robbie Ethridge and Charles Hudson, 177–223. Jackson: University Press of Mississippi.

Johnson, Samuel. 1755. *A Dictionary of the English Language: A Digital Edition.* Edited by Brandi Besalke. Last modified June 14, 2017. http://johnsonsdictionaryonline.com.

Kaye, Patricia. 1989. "'Women Are Alcoholics and Drug Addicts,' Says Dictionary." *ELT Journal* 43 (3): 192–95.

Klopotek, Brian. 2011. *Recognition Odysseys: Indigeneity, Race, and Federal Tribal Recognition Policy in Three Louisiana Indian Communities.* Durham, N.C.: Duke University Press.

Klopotek, Brian, John D. Barbry, Donna M. Pierite, and Elisabeth Pierite-Mora, eds. 2017. *The Tunica-Biloxi Tribe, Its Culture and People,* 2nd ed. Marksville: Tunica-Biloxi Tribe of Louisiana.

Kniffen, Fred B., Hiram F. Gregory, and George A. Stokes. 1994. *The Historic Indian Tribes of Louisiana: From 1542 to the Present.* Baton Rouge: Louisiana State University Press.

Krabill, Ron. 2012. "Graduate Mentoring against Common Sense." In *Collaborative Futures: Critical Reflections on Publicly Active Graduate Education,* edited by Amanda Gilvin, Georgia M. Roberts, and Craig Martin, 285–99. Syracuse, N.Y.: Syracuse University Press.

Kroskrity, Paul V., and Margaret C. Field, eds. 2009. *Native American Language Ideologies: Beliefs, Practices, and Struggles in Indian Country.* Tucson: University of Arizona Press.

KYLY (Kuhpani Yoyani Luhchi Yoroni). 2011. *Tayak Takohkuman (and) Hichut'una Awachihk'unanahch.* Marksville: Tunica-Biloxi Tribe of Louisiana.

KYLY (Kuhpani Yoyani Luhchi Yoroni). Forthcoming. *Tunica Textbook.* Bloomington: Indiana University Press.

Langley, Bertney, Linda Langley, Jack Martin, and Stephanie Hasselbacher. 2018. "The Koasati Language Project: A Collaborative, Community-Based Language Documentation and Revitalization Model." In Bischoff and Jany 2018, 132–50.

Laufer, Batia. 1992. "Corpus-Based Versus Lexicographer Examples in Comprehension and Production of New Words." In *EURALEX '92 Proceedings I–II*, edited by Hannu Tommola, Krista Varantola, Tarja Salmi-Tolonen, and Jürgen Schopp, 71–76. Tampere, Finland: University of Tampere.

Laufer, Batia. 1993. "The Effect of Dictionary Definitions and Examples on the Use and Comprehension of New L2 Words." *Cahiers de lexicologie* 63 (2): 131–42.

Le Page du Pratz, Simon. (1763) 1947. *The History of Louisiana, or of the Western Parts of Virginia and Carolina.* Reprinted, New Orleans: Pelican Press.

Leech, Geoffrey, and Hilary Nesi. 1999. "Moving towards Perfection: The Learners' (Electronic) Dictionary of the Future." In *The Perfect Learners' Dictionary (?),* edited by Thomas Herbst and Kerstin Popp, 295–308. Tübingen: Max Niemeyer Verlag.

Leonard, Wesley Y. 2018. "Reflections on (De)Colonialism in Language Documentation." In *Reflections on Language Documentation 20 Years after Himmelmann 1998.* Language Documentation and Conservation Special Publication no. 15, edited by Bradley McDonnell, Andrea L. Berez-Kroeker, and Gary Holton, 55–65. Honolulu: University of Hawai'i Press.

Leonard, Wesley Y., and Erin Haynes. 2010. "Making 'Collaboration' Collaborative: An Examination of Perspectives That Frame Linguistic Field Research." *Language Documentation and Conservation* 4:268–93.

Lew, Robert, and Joanna Doroszewska. 2009. "Electronic Dictionary Entries with Animated Pictures: Lookup Preference and Word Retention." *International Journal of Lexicography* 22 (3): 239–57.

Lin, Hua. 2003. "The Necessity of Output-Output Correspondence: Evidence from Tunica." *USC Working Papers in Linguistics* 1:29–47. http://gsil.sc-ling.org/wp-content /uploads/2009/01/2003_3_lin.pdf.

Lynch, Jack. 2009. *The Lexicographer's Dilemma: The Evolution of "Proper" English from Shakespeare to South Park.* New York: Bloomsbury.

Martin, Jack B. 2004. "Languages." In *Handbook of North American Indians,* vol. 14, *Southeast,* edited by Raymond D. Fogelson, 68–86. Washington, D.C.: Smithsonian.

Maxwell, Judith M. 2004. "Ownership of Indigenous Languages: A Case Study from Guatemala." In *Indigenous Intellectual Property Rights: Legal Obstacles and Innovative Solutions,* edited by Mary Riley, 173–215. Oxford: Altamira Press.

Maxwell, Judith M., Patricia Anderson, and Raina Heaton. 2017. "Tunica Language Revitalization." In Klopotek, Barbry, Pierite, and Pierite-Mora 2017, 45–48.

McDonald, Mary Anne. n.d. "Practicing Community-Engaged Research." Duke Center for Community Research. Accessed February 19, 2019. https://www.citiprogram.org/citi documents/Duke%20Med/Practicing/comm-engaged-research-4.pdf.

McKean, Erin. 2007. "The Joy of Lexicography." Filmed March 2007. TED video, 15:47. https://www.ted.com/talks/erin_mckean_redefines_the_dictionary.

McLendon, Sally. 1997. "Mary R. Haas: A Life in Linguistics." *Anthropological Linguistics* 39 (4): 522–43.

Medlicott, Carol. 2003. "Re-Thinking Geographical Exploration as Intelligence Collection: The Example of Lewis and Clark's 'Corps of Discovery.'" *Terra Incognitae* 35 (1): 54–68.

Merriam-Webster. 2017. "We Just Added More Than 1,000 New Words to the Dictionary." https://www.merriam-webster.com/words-at-play/new-words-in-the-dictionary-feb-2017.

Miromaa. n.d.a. "About Us." Accessed October 11, 2019. https://www.miromaa.org.au.

Miromaa. n.d.b. *Miromaa: Language Archiving, Collating and Resource Creation.* Newcastle, Australia: Arwarbukarl Cultural Resource Association. https://www.miromaa.org.au/images/files/miromaa/infobrochsm.pdf.

Mithun, Marianne. 1999. *The Languages of Native North America.* Cambridge: Cambridge University Press.

Montler, Timothy. 2012. *Klallam Dictionary.* Seattle: University of Washington Press.

Mugglestone, Lynda. 2011. *Dictionaries: A Very Short Introduction.* New York: Oxford University Press.

Munro, Pamela. 2002. "Entries for Verbs in American Indian Language Dictionaries." In Frawley, Hill, and Munro 2002, 86–107.

Nettle, Daniel, and Suzanne Romaine. 2002. *Vanishing Voices: The Extinction of the World's Languages.* New York: Oxford University Press.

Newman, Paul, and Martha Susan Ratliff, eds. 2001. *Linguistic Fieldwork.* Cambridge: Cambridge University Press.

Ogawa, Kunihiko. 1971. "A Generative Transformational Study of Tunica Syntax." PhD diss., University of Utah.

Ogilvie, Sarah, ed. 2011a. "Dictionaries of Endangered Languages." Special issue, *International Journal of Lexicography* 24 (4).

Ogilvie, Sarah. 2011b. "Linguistics, Lexicography, and the Revitalization of Endangered Languages." In Ogilvie 2011a, 389–404.

O'Shannessy, Carmel. 2011. "Language Contact and Change in Endangered Languages." In *The Cambridge Handbook of Endangered Languages*, edited by Peter K. Austin and Julia Sallabank, 78–99. Cambridge: Cambridge University Press.

Ostermann, Carolin. 2015. *Cognitive Lexicography: A New Approach to Lexicography Making Use of Cognitive Semantics.* Berlin: De Gruyter.

Oxford Dictionaries. 2014. "How Do New Words Get Added to Oxford Dictionaries?" Uploaded August 14, 2014. YouTube, 2:00. https://www.youtube.com/watch?v=juwDkP3ovIY.

Oxford Dictionaries. 2018. "How Many Words Are There in the English Language?" https://en.oxforddictionaries.com/explore/how-many-words-are-there-in-the-english-language.

Oxford English Dictionary. 2014. "New Words List June 2014." https://public.oed.com/updates/new-words-list-june-2014.

Oxford English Dictionary. n.d.a. "Frequently Asked Questions." Accessed February 21, 2019. https://public.oed.com/help.

Oxford English Dictionary. n.d.b. "Top 1000 Sources." Accessed February 26, 2019. http://
www.oed.com/.

Oxford English Dictionary. n.d.c. "History of the OED." Accessed June 6, 2020. https://
public.oed.com/history/.

Peters, Robert A. 1968. "Robert Cawdrey and the First English Dictionary." *Journal of
English Linguistics* 2 (1): 29–42.

Pierite, Joseph. 1964. Letter to Mary Haas. Mary Rosamond Haas Papers, Mss.Ms.Coll.94.
American Philosophical Society Library, Philadelphia, Pa.

Postma, Julie. 2008. "Balancing Power among Academic and Community Partners: The
Case of El Proyecto Bienestar." *Journal of Empirical Research on Human Research Ethics*
3 (2): 17–32.

Preston, Dennis R. 2002. "The Story of Good and Bad English in the United States." In
Alternative Histories of English, edited by Richard J. Watts and Peter Trudgill, 134–52.
London: Routledge.

Ptasznik, Bartosz. 2013. "Entry-Internal Navigation in Dictionaries: A Review of the Literature." *Acta Neophilologica* 15 (2): 177–90.

Pulte, William, and Durbin Feeling. 2002. "Morphology in Cherokee Lexicography: The
Cherokee English Dictionary." In Frawley, Hill, and Munro 2002, 60–69.

Quintero, Carolyn. 2014. *Osage Dictionary*. Norman: University of Oklahoma Press.

Rafael, Vincent L. (1993) 2001. *Contracting Colonialism: Translation and Christian Conver-
sion in Tagalog Society under Early Spanish Rule*. Durham, N.C.: Duke University Press.

Rice, Keren. 2011. "Documentary Linguistics and Community Relations." *Language Documentation and Conservation* 5:187–207.

Rice, Keren. 2018. "Collaborative Research: Visions and Realities." In Bischoff and Jany
2018, 13–37.

Rice, Keren, and Leslie Saxon. 2002. "Issues of Standardization and Community in Aboriginal Language Lexicography." In Frawley, Hill, and Munro 2002, 125–54.

Robertson, Jamie. n.d. "Dictionary Stand." Artful Home. Accessed February 7, 2019.
https://www.artfulhome.com/product/Wood-Dictionary-Stand/Dictionary-Stand
/15566.

Ross, Jane F., Fabrice Jaumont, Julia Schulz, Joseph Dunn, and Lauren Ducrey. 2018. "Sustainability of French Heritage Language Education in the United States." In *Handbook
of Research and Practice in Heritage Language Education*, edited by Peter Pericles Trifonas
and Themistoklis Aravossitas, 731–48. Berlin: Springer.

Rundell, Michael. 1999. "Dictionary Use in Production." *International Journal of Lexicography*. 12 (1): 35–53.

Saltmarsh, John, Dwight E. Giles Jr., Elaine Ward, and Suzanne M. Buglione. 2009.
"Rewarding Community-Engaged Scholarship." *New Directions for Higher Education*
147:25–35.

Sapir, Edward. 1921. *Language: An Introduction to the Study of Speech.* New York: Harcourt Brace.

Schensul, Stephen L., Jean J. Schensul, Merrill Singer, Margaret Weeks, and Marie Brault. 2015. "Participatory Methods and Community-Based Collaboration." In *Handbook of Methods in Cultural Anthropology,* edited by H. Russell Bernard and Clarence C. Gravlee, 185–212. London: Rowman and Littlefield.

Scholfield, Phil. 1999. "Dictionary Use in Reception." *International Journal of Lexicography.* 12 (1): 13–34.

Schryver, Gilles-Maurice de. 2003. "Lexicographers' Dreams in the Electronic-Dictionary Age." *International Journal of Lexicography* 16 (10): 143–99.

Shore, Nancy, Kristine Wong, Sarena D. Seifer, Jessica Gingon, and Vanessa N. Gamble. 2008. "Introduction to Special Issue: Advancing the Ethics of Community-Based Participatory Research." *Journal of Empirical Research on Human Research Ethics* 3 (2): 1–4.

Sibley, John. 1832. "Historical Sketches of the Several Indian Tribes in Louisiana, South of the Arkansas River, and Between the Mississippi and River Grande. Communicated to Congress by Thomas Jefferson, February 19, 1806." *American State Papers: Indian Affairs* 1:721–30.

SIL International. 2015. "SIL Terms of Service for Webonary.org." Last modified October 6, 2015. https://www.webonary.org/sil-international-terms-of-service-for-webonary-org.

SIL International. 2020. "Dictionary App Builder." Accessed June 18, 2020. http://software.sil.org/dictionaryappbuilder.

SIL International. n.d. "About." Accessed October 12, 2019. https://www.sil.org/about.

Sinclair, John McH. 2003. "Corpora for Lexicography." In Sterkenburg 2003, 167–78.

Skinner, David. 2012. *The Story of Ain't: America, Its Language, and the Most Controversial Dictionary Ever Published.* New York: Harper Collins.

Smith, Linda Tuhiwai. 2012. *Decolonizing Methodologies: Research and Indigenous Peoples.* London: Zed Books.

Sterkenburg, Piet van, ed. 2003. *A Practical Guide to Lexicography.* Amsterdam: John Benjamins.

Svensén, Bo. 1993. *Practical Lexicography: Principles and Methods of Dictionary Making.* Oxford: Oxford University Press.

Svensén, Bo. 2009. *A Handbook of Lexicography: The Theory and Practice of Dictionary-Making.* Cambridge: Cambridge University Press.

Swanepoel, Piet. 1994. "Problems, Theories and Methodologies in Current Lexicographic Semantic Research." In *Proceedings of the 6th EURALEX International Congress,* edited by Willy Martin, Willem Meijs, Margreet Moerland, Elsemiek ten Pas, Piet van Sterkenburg, and Piek Vossen, 11–26. Amsterdam: EURALEX.

Swanton, John R. 1911. *Indian Tribes of the Lower Mississippi Valley and Adjacent Coast of the Gulf of Mexico.* Washington, D.C.: Bureau of American Ethnology.

Swanton, John R. 1919. *A Structural and Lexical Comparison of the Tunica, Chitimacha, and Atakapa Languages*. Washington, D.C.: Bureau of American Ethnology.

Swanton, John R. 1921. "The Tunica Language." *International Journal of American Linguistics* 2:1–39.

Swanton, John R. 1931. *Source Material for the Social and Ceremonial Life of the Choctaw Indians*. Washington, D.C.: Bureau of American Ethnology.

Swanton, John R. n.d. Swanton Manuscripts. National Anthropological Archives, Smithsonian Institution, Washington, D.C.

Tarp, Sven. 2000. "Theoretical Challenges to LSP Lexicography." *Lexikos* 10:189–208.

Tarp, Sven. 2002. "Translation Dictionaries and Bilingual Dictionaries. Two Different Concepts." *Journal of Translation Studies* 7:59–84.

Tarp, Sven. 2008. *Lexicography in the Borderland between Knowledge and Non-Knowledge. General Lexicographical Theory with Particular Focus on Learner's Lexicography*. Tübingen, Germany: De Gruyter.

Tarp, Sven. 2011. "Lexicographical and Other e-Tools for Consultation Purposes: Towards the Individualization of Needs Satisfaction." In Fuertes-Olivera and Bergenholtz 2011, 54–70.

Tarp, Sven. 2012. "Do We Need a (New) Theory of Lexicography?" *Lexikos* 22:321–32.

Thieberger, Nick. (1995) 2005. *Paper and Talk: A Manual for Reconstituting Materials in Australian Indigenous Languages from Historical Sources*. Canberra: Aboriginal Studies Press.

Thieberger, Nick. 2011. "Building a Lexical Database with Multiple Outputs: Examples from Legacy Data and Multimodal Fieldwork." In Ogilvie 2011a, 463–72.

Thwaites, Reuben Gold, ed. 1896. *The Jesuit Relations and Allied Documents: Travels and Explorations of the Jesuit Missionaries in New France, 1610–1791*. Vol. 65, *Lower Canada, Mississippi Valley, 1696–1702*. Cleveland, Ohio: Burrows Brothers.

Toelken, Barre. 1998. "The Yellowman Tapes, 1966–1997." *Journal of American Folklore* 111 (442): 381–91.

Tono, Yukio. 1984. "On the Dictionary User's Reference Skills." BEd thesis, Gakugei University, Tokyo.

Tunica-Biloxi Tribe of Louisiana. 2020. *Tunica–English Dictionary*. Last updated April 13, 2020. https://www.webonary.org/tunica/.

Tunica-Tulane Working Group. 2011. *Hichut'una Awachihk'unanahch Fighting Eagles/Tayak Takohkuman Deer and Turtle*. Stories told to Mary Haas by Sesostrie Youchigant in Tunica. Edited by Judith M. Maxwell, Kat Bell, Raina Heaton, John de Priest, Joshua Rogers, and Rebecca Chilbert. Marksville, La.: Tunica Nation.

Turin, Mark. 2016. "Ethnoscape: Tools and Technologies for Language Mobilization and Cultural Revitalization in First Nations Communities." Presented at the Translating across Time and Space symposium, American Philosophical Society, Philadelphia, Pa., October 14, 2016.

Ulrich, Heidi. 2011. "Electronic Dictionaries as Tools: Toward an Assessment of Usability." In Fuertes-Olivera and Bergenholtz 2011, 287–304.

UNESCO Ad Hoc Expert Group on Endangered Languages. 2003. *Language Vitality and Endangerment.* Document submitted to the International Expert Meeting on UNESCO Programme Safeguarding of Endangered Languages, Paris, March 10–12, 2003.

Warner, Natasha, Lynnika Butler, and Quirina Luna-Costillas. 2006. "Making a Dictionary for Community Use in Language Revitalization: The Case of Mutsun." *International Journal of Lexicography* 19 (3): 257–85.

Warner, Natasha, Quirina Luna, and Lynnika Butler. 2007. "Ethics and Revitalization of Dormant Languages: The Mutsun Language." *Language Documentation and Conservation* 1 (1): 58–76.

Warner, Natasha, Quirina Luna, Lynnika Butler, and Heather Van Volkinburg. 2009. "Revitalization in a Scattered Language Community: Problems and Methods from the Perspective of Mutsun Language Revitalization." *International Journal of Sociology and Language* 198:135–48.

Wilson, Aidan. 2010. "Electronic Dictionaries for Language Reclamation." In *Re-Awakening Languages: Theory and Practice in the Revitalisation of Australia's Indigenous Languages,* edited by John Hobson, Kevin Lowe, Susan Poetsch, and Michael Walsh, 339–48. Sydney: Sydney University Press.

Wisecup, Kelly. 2016. "From National Collections to Decolonial Archives: Cherokee Interventions in Language Collecting." Presented at the Translating across Time and Space symposium, American Philosophical Society, Philadelphia, Pa, October 15, 2016.

Wiswall, Wendy J. 1991. "Tunica Partial Vowel Harmony as Support for a Height Node." *Arizona Phonology Conference* 4:88–112.

Yurok Language Project. 2017. Yurok Language Project Digital Archive. http://corpus.linguistics.berkeley.edu/~yurok/index.php.

Zgusta, Ladislav. 1971. *Manual of Lexicography.* Prague: Czechoslovak Academy of Sciences.

Zlotkowski, Edward. 1999. "Pedagogy and Engagement." In *Colleges and Universities as Citizens,* edited by Robert G. Bringle and E. A. Malloy, 96–120. Boston: Allyn and Bacon.

Index

About the Author

Patricia M. Anderson holds a PhD in linguistic anthropology from Tulane University. She is an active member of the Tunica Language Project and head lexicographer of the New Tunica Dictionary. Her research focuses on language revitalization in Native North America and the intersection of language revitalization and technology. When not working on language projects, Anderson builds computer software and wrestles with her toddler.

Printed and bound by CPI Group (UK) Ltd, Croydon, CR0 4YY

06/07/2026

02160599-0002